Struggle and Suffrage
in
Chelmsford

Struggle and Suffrage
in
Chelmsford

Women's Lives and the Fight for Equality

Stephen Wynn

PEN & SWORD
HISTORY

AN IMPRINT OF PEN & SWORD BOOKS LTD
YORKSHIRE · PHILADELPHIA

First published in Great Britain in 2019 by
Pen & Sword History
An imprint of
Pen & Sword Books Limited
Yorkshire - Philadelphia

Copyright © Stephen Wynn, 2019

ISBN 978 1 52671 6 064

A CIP catalogue record for this book is available from the British Library

Typeset in 11.5/14 point Times New Roman
by Aura Technology and Software Services, India

Printed and bound in the UK
by 4edge Ltd, Essex, SS5 4AD

Pen & Sword Books Limited incorporates the imprints of Atlas,
Archaeology, Aviation, Discovery, Family History, Fiction, History, Maritime,
Military, Military Classics, Politics, Select, Transport, True Crime, Air World,
Frontline Publishing, Leo Cooper, Remember When, Seaforth Publishing,
The Praetorian Press, Wharncliffe Local History, Wharncliffe Transport,
Wharncliffe True Crime and White Owl.

For a complete list of Pen & Sword titles please contact
PEN & SWORD BOOKS LIMITED
47 Church Street, Barnsley, South Yorkshire S70 2AS, United Kingdom
E-mail: enquiries@pen-and-sword.co.uk
Website: www.pen-and-sword.co.uk

Or
PEN AND SWORD BOOKS
1950 Lawrence Rd, Havertown, PA 19083, USA
E-mail: Uspen-and-sword@casematepublishers.com
Website: www.penandswordbooks.com

Contents

CHAPTER ONE

Women's Health

The Contagious Diseases Act 1864 was brought in to deal with the growing number of cases of members of the armed forces contracting venereal diseases through their contact with prostitutes. Official figures show that by 1864, one out of every three cases of a soldier reporting sick was related to a venereal disease from a prostitute. The problems were much worse in and around garrison towns where there were large numbers of young soldiers with time on their hands and money to spend, especially on Friday and Saturday nights. The problem became so bad that the original Act required further amendments in 1866 and 1869.

The original 1864 Act allowed police to arrest women they suspected of working as prostitutes, but only in certain towns that had naval ports or were established Army garrison towns. By 1869 however, the number of specified towns had risen to eighteen. Once arrested, the women were then subjected to compulsory examinations, to see if they were infected with any form of venereal disease. If they were, they could be confined in what was called a lock hospital, which was simply a medical facility that specialised in the treatment of venereal diseases. There they would remain until their treatment was complete and they were free of the disease. The original Act of 1864 allowed for women to be detained for up to three months, but by 1869, lessons had been learnt, and the period of time a woman could be detained had been increased to a year. A problem with these lock hospitals, or rather the voluntary ones, was that there wasn't enough of them. In 1882, it was estimated that there were 402 beds for female patients, but only 232 of these were available for use at any given time. The only other option for women who believed they may have contracted a venereal disease was to take themselves off to their local workhouse infirmary.

A good analogy would be to compare, say, the proven health risks associated with smoking compared with the costs to the NHS of treating related illnesses. The government still won't ban smoking because of the large sum of money it receives in the way of tax from the sales of tobacco related items.

Prostitutes were seen as a necessary evil, soldiers were often unmarried and acts of homosexuality constituted a criminal offence. Both senior military personnel and members of the medical world saw the detaining of prostitutes in lock hospitals as an effective means of helping prevent the spread of venereal diseases.

One of the main stumbling blocks, as far as reformists and other individuals who possessed a balanced and, let's say, a more forward thinking approach to such matters, questioned why there was no provision in the Act for the examination of prostitutes' clients who, common sense suggested, were just as guilty of the spreading of venereal diseases as the prostitutes themselves. This very point became a major bone of contention in the campaign to repeal the Contagious Diseases Acts.

In some ways, the debate just highlighted the inequality between the two sexes and became the touch paper which ignited the flame for women organising themselves and to begin actively campaigning for their rights.

Josephine Elizabeth Butler was a feminist and a social reformer and in 1869 she became involved in the campaign to repeal the Contagious Diseases Acts, which was finally achieved in 1886. According to an article on Wikipedia, in one of her public letters on the matter she included a personal account by a prostitute on her dealings with men. What the woman said was profound:

It is men, only men, from the first to the last that we have to do with! To please a man I did wrong at first, then I was flung about from man to man. Men Police lay hands upon us. By men we are examined, handled, doctored. In the hospital it is a man again who makes prayer and reads the bible for us. We are had up before the magistrates who are men, and we never get out of the hands of men till we die.

Victorian England was awash with large numbers of prostitutes, possibly a reflection of the utter destitution and feelings of helplessness these women found themselves in. The majority of prostitutes were from the working classes, women who had little in the way of an education in their formative years, and prostitution was simply the best way they had of earning a living, despite the inherent dangers that went with the job. Most of the jobs that would have been available to them would have meant working extremely long hours for a very poor wage. Complain, and the likelihood would have been the sack.

One of the main problems of dealing with the spreading of venereal diseases by prostitutes, was nobody really knew just how many there were. There were estimations made by different organisations, but how much value they had was questionable. Even the police could only go on the number of prostitutes they arrested for the figures which they produced. For every one that was arrested, there might be three, four, five, or more that never came to their attention, and there in part lay the problem.

An example of just how difficult life was shown on Tuesday 6 May 1913 when the body of 44-year-old Mary Winifed Brett, born in Chelmsford in 1869, and a single woman who lived at 52 Lower Street, Chelmsford, was found in the River Wid. An inquest into her death heard from Father Shepherd, the priest at the Church of the Immaculate Conception, Chelmsford, who knew the deceased quite well. He had seen her the previous afternoon outside Oaklands on London Road. He got off his bicycle and enquired how she was as, besides being a nice person, he knew that she had recently been suffering with her nerves and had previously suffered a breakdown, which she was still recovering from. She appeared quite cheerful, and told Father Shepherd that she was feeling much better within herself and hoped that she would soon be better. Her demeanour seemed positive and he didn't notice anything odd or unusual about her manner.

Sergeant Smith, stationed at Widford Police station, told the inquest that at 5.45 pm on the evening of Monday, 5 May 1913 he had searched the bank of the River Wid which, he added, was in full flood. After a short search he discovered a lady's hat, gloves and other articles. The following morning, having received information that Mary Winifred Brett was missing and had been since the previous morning, he decided to drag the river close to the spot where he had found the items the previous afternoon. About 500 yards away from where the items had been discovered, and in about 4 feet of water, Sergeant Smith and a constable discovered a woman's body, which was later confirmed to be that of Mary Winifred Brett. A Mr Cedric Richards, who was a lodger at the deceased's house, identified her body.

The jury at the inquest further heard from Dr T.H. Waller, who had been treating Mary Winifred for between three and four months, who provided evidence that she had been suffering from nervous debility. However, she had never displayed any suicidal tendencies when he had seen her. The coroner asked 'In cases of this sort, these tendencies suddenly develop, do they not?' Dr Waller replied 'Oh yes. The deceased was always depressed and generally miserable, but never talked enough to suggest that she was contemplating suicide.'

In summing up, the coroner said that there could be no doubt that the deceased drowned herself, and a verdict of suicide during temporary insanity was returned.

By today's standards in such matters, I am not sure that the same verdict would have been so readily returned. Just because there were no obvious signs of a struggle, it does not preclude the possibility that foul play was a factor in Mary's death. Having said that, and accepting Mary's death was one of suicide, I am not sure whether her death reflects more on the poor state of health care at the time, especially for those who maybe were not so affluent, or the harshness of how life was for a large majority of people, who simply couldn't cope. Sadly, for some of those, the only way out, was death.

I searched the census records from 1871 to 1911 and found no trace of a Mary Winifred Brett. However, I did find a record confirming her birth in 1869 in Chelmsford.

An inquest was opened by the coroner, Mr L.F. Beccle, at the Shire Hall on Saturday, 10 December 1938 into the death of Mrs Amelia Elizabeth Burdett, who was 56 years of age and who lived at Baddow Road, Chelmsford, with her husband, Charles Burdett. She had, according to local newspaper reports, taken her own life by placing her head in the oven and turning on all the gas taps. She was found by her husband, Charles, who was an unemployed labourer. He told the inquest that his late wife had been a voluntary patient at the Severalls Mental Hospital, a psychiatric hospital in Colchester, which had opened in 1910 and could cater for a maximum of 2,000 patients. By all accounts it was a hellish place, where psychiatrists were basically free to carry out experiments on their patients. This included Electro Convulsive Therapy (ECT) and frontal lobotomy, both of which were still being used in the 1950s. In a 1998 book by Diana Gittins, *Madness in its Place: Narratives of Severalls Hospital, 1913–1997,* she explains how women were sometimes admitted by their own families, for reasons as varied as having been raped, having had an illegitimate child, or not being able to carry out daily tasks.

Mrs Burdett had only been discharged from the hospital three weeks before her death, after having spent five weeks as a patient there. She had suffered with depression and did not sleep well.

At 2.30 pm on Saturday, 10 December 1938 Charles Burdett went out to do some shopping and asked Amelia if she might like to go with him. She politely declined, saying that she would stay at home and rest. He returned home just before 5 pm, and as soon as he opened the front door he could smell the gas. He called out to his wife that she had left the gas on, but she did not reply, so he went to the gas meter and turned off the supply. He then went into the kitchen and found his wife lying on her back with her head in the open oven. She was already dead.

Asked by the coroner if he could offer any explanation as to why his wife would have acted in such a way. Mr Burdett replied that on Thursday, 15 December 1938 he and his wife were due to move into a bungalow, and although she was looking forward to the move, she was also worried about the upheaval.

Dr F.E. Camps gave evidence that Mrs Burdett had died due to carbon monoxide poisoning.

On Monday, 8 September 1947 Mrs Doris Davies, of Bishop Road, Chelmsford, the wife of a well-known employee of the town's Marconi factory, which had built radios for all arms of the military during the war, was found dead in the gas-filled kitchen of her house. Mrs Davies and her husband were described as a happy couple. Only the day before her death, the couple had enjoyed an outing together to the seaside town of Southend.

The inquest took place in Chelmsford the day after her death. The court heard how she could become depressed quite quickly and for no apparent reason. Her husband told the jury that she was a worrier by nature, and what most people found trivial, would greatly play on her mind. They were and always had been an extremely happy couple who had no financial or other worries. They had a 19-year-old daughter who they both loved and she was in full-time employment. He could offer no explanation as to why she would have chosen to taker her own life, and he was shocked and numb at her loss.

Having heard all the evidence the jury decided that Mrs Davis had killed herself while the balance of her mind was disturbed.

Mrs Davies, as far as her friends and family were concerned, had an ideal life. Nobody could have foreseen how her life was going to end, because to them everything in her world was as perfect as it could possibly be. But this was a time for both men and women, where talking about issues or problems, wasn't the norm or the done thing to do. It was still a world where people just got on with their lives. There was a 'snap out of it' type of attitude and most definitely not a consoling arm around the shoulder type of concern.

The sad thing for Mrs Davies was that she had people who loved her and thought the world about her. But she felt unable, for whatever reason, to reach out to them and for them it was a case of just not seeing or reading the signs. So sad, and such a shame.

It has always been intriguing to me why people do certain things, especially when their motive for doing it isn't immediately obvious. Sometimes it can be down to the day-to-day pressures of life, sometimes it is out of need or even down to the simple fact that they can get away with it. This next example, I found particularly interesting.

On Monday, 27 October 1924, Mr Arthur Hugh Brown, who was an officer in the Mercantile Marine, or what would today be known as the Merchant Navy, petitioned in the Divorce Court before Mr Justice Horridge, for the marriage to his wife, Florence Ellen Brown, to be dissolved on the grounds of her adultery with an unnamed man. The suit was not defended.

Mr Brown gave evidence that he and Florence had been married on 7 March 1916 in Chelmsford and lived together at Garden Cottage, Rectory Lane, Chelmsford, which was the home of Florence's parents.

Because of his line of work, Mr Brown was constantly away at sea for long periods, but when home on leave he always returned to see his wife. In November 1919 he was surprised at the condition she was in, as she was noticeably heavier in build than he remembered. Mr Brown later discovered that Florence had registered the birth of a child in his name. The couple met up again in March 1920 and Arthur questioned her about the child she had given birth to, possibly because he had worked out the dates when he had been home on leave, to see if he was the father or not. In reply Florence told him that she did not know who the father of the child was.

Mr Robert Andrew Michie, who was an officer at the Ministry of Pensions, but who was stationed at the naval base at Portland, confirmed that Arthur was not at home at the time when the child must have been conceived. He had worked with Arthur and seen him every day between January and December 1919.

Arthur was awarded a *decree nisi* by the judge. This was without doubt a difficult time for women and sex. Religion played a big part, as under the Church's direction, sex between a man and a woman wasn't for enjoyment and pleasure, but to conceive children within a marriage.

The first rubber condoms had been available since 1855 and were not only intended to prevent pregnancy, but also to help prevent the spread of sexually transmitted diseases. However, their use was not supported by the Church and this had a huge influence on society's attitudes. What woman in her right mind, or man for that matter, would try and purchase such an item? As far as the outside world was concerned, if you were a married couple then you should only be having sex in order to produce children, so the buying of such an item was going to leave the purchaser open to some difficult questions from members of their own community.

The first latex condoms were manufactured in the 1920s and the contraceptive pill for women was introduced in 1959. It was available on the NHS from 1961 but only to married women. But once again for devout Catholics it was a difficult choice to make.

The following example potentially shows the extremes that women would go to if faced with an unwanted pregnancy.

On 30 January 1854, a woman by the name of Bareham pleaded guilty to a charge of assaulting her illegitimate son. She had left home that day with the intention of going to the Chelmsford workhouse in Moulsham. Whether that was to deposit her son, or herself and her son, was not clear, but Mrs Bareham changed her mind on route and instead left her son behind a large heap of manure by the road side. Thankfully for the child, he was discovered by some passers-by. He would likely have died if not discovered, because of the winter weather.

Fortunately for Bareham, the child survived. She was charged with child abandonment rather than attempted murder. Her punishment was two years' imprisonment with hard labour, which in the circumstances was extremely fortuitous. What state of mind Bareham must have been in to carry out such a vile act can only be guessed at, but it seems that she wanted the child to die. Otherwise she would surely have dropped him off at the Chelmsford Union workhouse in Moulsham.

CHAPTER TWO

National Union of Women's Suffrage Societies

Before looking at the situation of women in Chelmsford between 1850 and 1950, I believe it is helpful to look at the subject of women's rights on a national level, as that will hopefully provide more perspective on the subject at a local level. But before I do that, an example of how difficult life could be for women in particular, especially from the lower classes. Life for everyday folk was a tough existence back in the 1850s especially in some of the big towns and cities throughout the country. For the people of Chelmsford, it was no different.

Prior to 1850 people's rights had been governed by what was known as Chartism; a working-class movement whose aim was political reform throughout the country. The movement was strongest in northern England, the East Midlands, Staffordshire, the Black Country and the valleys of South Wales, although it has to be said this was more relevant to men than it was for women, simply because men made up more of the working population at the time.

The age of reformism began during the nineteenth century and one of the movements that was part of that time was the feminist movement, or the women's movement, as it was also known. They campaigned on such issues as domestic violence, women's suffrage, and sexual violence.

The first organised movement for women's suffrage in Britain, was the 'Langham Place Circle', which began in the 1850s. Amongst those who were members of the organisation were Barbara Leigh Smith Bodichon, Emily Faithfull, Emily Davies and Bessie Rayner Parkes. The aims of the group were legal reform for women's status, women's employment, along with improved educational opportunities. They were responsible for producing a monthly periodical entitled the *English Woman's Journal*, that was published and sold between 1858 and 1864, at a cost of one shilling. From 1860 to 1864 the *Journal* was printed by Emily Faithfull, who had begun her own printing company in London called the Victoria Press, a business that employed women workers instead of men. This was not the norm back in 1860s Britain and was a decision which caused some controversy and one which brought her to the attention of the royal family.

Such was the standing and reputation of Emily Faithfull's work and of the Victoria Press, that she was appointed as the printer and publisher in ordinary to Queen Victoria, a remarkable achievement in a time when it was most definitely a man's world.

In 1863 she published a monthly magazine entitled the *Victoria Magazine*, which she used to advocate the claims of women to remunerative employment. She continued in this vein and lectured in both England and America on the subject of furthering the interests of women.

In 1864 Emily Faithfull became embroiled in the divorce of Admiral Henry Codrington and his wife Helen Jane Smith Codrington. It was a complicated matter, one that saw Codrington initially accused of attempting to rape Faithfull, an allegation that she refused to confirm by declining to provide a written testimony and the matter was dropped. Amidst the allegations and counter allegations of the divorce, it was even suggested that Emily Faithful and Helen Codrington were lesbian lovers. This was at a time where personal reputation was everything, without it, life in all its aspects could very quickly become quite an isolated existence.

A discussion group for women was formed in March 1865, the meetings of which were held at 44 Phillimore Gardens, Kensington,

London, the home of Charlotte Manning, which is situated just to the north of Kensington High Street. The name of the group was the Kensington Society, and at their first meeting eleven women were in attendance, although at its peak the group numbered sixty-seven in total.

Most of the women were single, well-educated and from the middle classes, and were looking to pursue careers in medicine, education and to better the cause of women in general. By way of example, Charlotte Manning was a feminist scholar as well as being the first head of Girton College at Cambridge University. Another member was Elizabeth Anderson, who went on to become the first woman in Britain to qualify as a physician and surgeon.

On 20 May 1867 a proposal was put forward in Parliament by John Stuart Mill, MP, that women should be granted the same rights as men. The proposal was defeated, and although seventy-three MPs had voted for it, which in itself was a remarkable achievement, the result was a disappointment to members of the Kensington Society, some of whom decided to form the London Society for Women's Suffrage. However, despite this setback the campaign for women's suffrage did not come to an end. The women continued their struggle in the hope and belief that they would eventually make a difference. By the 1890s there were at least seventeen separate suffrage groups operating in different parts of the country.

Individual groups failed to make great strides towards securing women's suffrage, despite the determination of group members. On 14 October 1897, all the different groups, which in essence meant the National Central Society for Women's Suffrage, and the Central Committee, National Society for Women's Society, united and became the National Union of Women's Suffrage Societies (NUWSS). Its aims were to achieve women's suffrage through peaceful and legal means. The two groups had previously been united, but had split and gone their own ways in 1888.

The newly formed, or rather re-formed NUWSS, united under the leadership of Dame Millicent Garrett Fawcett, who was an intellectual, activist and writer. To some she was a feminist icon.

In 1901 she was appointed to lead the British Government's commission to South Africa to investigate conditions within the concentration camps that had come about as a result of the Second Boer War. Her report highlighted just how poorly run the camps were, and the appalling conditions in which people were held.

She remained the group's President until 1919. Although she was a tireless campaigner for women's rights, particularly when it came to improving women's opportunities in receiving a higher education, she was also a moderate who did not advocate violence or extremism to achieve her aims.

One of the issues in relation to women's rights was their status in a relationship. As I have written about elsewhere in this book, the children of a marriage belonged to the father, so in any divorce, regardless of how abusive the man might have been to his wife, it was normal practice for the children to stay with their father, assuming of course that he wanted them. But to some extent this highlighted the potential problem for women if they found themselves stuck in what had become an abusive marriage. Unlike today when domestic violence is high on the agenda for police forces across the country, in the latter years of the nineteenth century, a woman was seen as the property of her husband, for him to do with what he wanted, within reason.

A sad example of the extremes of an abusive relationship is shown in the following example.

On Tuesday, 5 December 1899, Samuel Crozier was hanged for the murder of his wife at Galleywood on 25 June 1899. He had previously been a publican in Chelmsford – as recently as 1895 he had been the landlord at the Globe Inn – and was relatively well-known around the town. The records show that Crozier slept well the night before his execution, and awoke at 6.20 am before eating a hearty breakfast. At 7 am he was visited by the prison chaplain, who took his last confession and then stayed with him till the end.

As was normal on such occasions, the tolling of the prison bell began at 7.45 am, the sombre sound echoing loudly along the concrete landings of the prison, each of the prisoners knowing full well its meaning.

At 7.55 am, Crozier was just five minutes from death. The High Sheriff of Essex, accompanied by the executioner, Mr James Billington, entered his cell. There was no struggle from the condemned man, who it would appear had accepted his fate, as Billington fastened his arms firmly behind his back. The High Sheriff asked Crozier if he had any last words that he wanted recording. He replied, '*No sir; no, nothing more than I have said.*' The High Sheriff and Billington then led the way to the execution chamber, just a few yards away. Prison warders stood either side of Crozier, with the chaplain, prayer book open in his hands, bringing up the rear. As he approached the scaffold Billington strapped Crozier's legs tightly together, then adjusted the rope loosely around his neck before placing a white cap over his head. There was an eerie silence about the proceedings, made even more surreal by the calmness of the condemned man as he was about to meet his maker. As the time finally reached 8 am, Billington gave a gentle tug of the lever, the trapdoor opened, and after a drop of seven feet, Crozier was dead. The fracturing of his neck resulted in an instantaneous death.

The cold, damp, misty weather had not been a sufficient deterrent to prevent a large crowd from gathering outside to watch the black flag, which signified Crozier's death, hoisted high above the prison gates.

An inquest, held later that same day in the prison by the coroner, Mr Lewes, confirmed the time and cause of Crozier's death.

Samuel Crozier was 53 years of age at the time of his execution. Although for many years he had been the landlord of the Globe Inn at Chelmsford, by the end of 1898 he was out of work but still living in the area. At about the same time he met a woman, Cecilia Jane Savage, who at 31 years of age was considerably younger than him. She worked as a barmaid at the Fleece Inn, Duke Street, Chelmsford. They quickly became romantically acquainted and on 7 January 1899 they were married at Chelmsford parish church, before moving in to lodgings in Victoria Road.

It very quickly became apparent to anybody who knew them, that Crozier had begun physically ill-treating his wife. In March 1899 they moved and went to live at the Admiral Rous Inn, a public house where Crozier was the new landlord. It was situated no more than 100 yards from the grandstand of the Chelmsford Racecourse at Galleywood. The move had not changed Crozier's behaviour, or prevented his acts of violence towards his wife of less than a year. Instead, his acts of violence towards her increased in their severity, and on several occasions she was seen to have a black eye, or be suffering from bruises to her arms and shoulders. On Sunday 25 June 1899 these violent acts of aggression and brutality culminated in the tragic events which saw Crozier's life ended on the gallows at Chelmsford prison.

Early that morning Mrs Crozier was seen to be in some distress. She had two black eyes and her lip was cut; she looked as though she had been given a sound beating by her errant husband. Throughout the course of the day Crozier appeared to be somewhat excited, but for no obvious reason. During the morning he was heard telling some people that his first wife had died in a lunatic asylum, and that this one was a lot worse, and that the sooner she went there the better it would be for her. Not satisfied with that vilification of his wife, he added that he would 'do for her before night'.

The bar of the Admiral Rous Inn faced the front of the premises, and it would appear that the blinds in those front-facing windows were not drawn, which allowed several people to look through them during the evening and witness the final acts of brutality carried out by Crozier on his defenceless wife, which directly led to her death. Despite there having been several people who witnessed the actual murder, only one person tried to intervene and remonstrate with Crozier, trying to stop him from doing further harm to his wife.

Crozier was seen to physically lift his wife from the sofa on which she was reclining, in what was described as a half-dazed condition, and then force her violently back down. He then picked her up and threw her back with such force that she fell off the sofa and landed heavily on the floor. Rather than go to her assistance, he simply walked out of the room, leaving her where she had fallen, and didn't return for some hours, when he was seen to enter the same room holding a lighted lamp. His wife was still lying on the floor where he had previously left her. He was seen to kick her and leave her where she was. The light of his lamp appeared in the bedroom window a matter of seconds later.

The following morning Mrs Crozier was found in the same position she had been left in the previous evening, which was a Sunday.

Crozier's story at his wife's subsequent inquest was that he had left her on the sofa on the Sunday night, and that she had drunk far too much, but promised to follow him to bed. He further stated that he and his wife were on good terms. Medical evidence somewhat contradicted this claim, revealing that Cecilia's body was covered in bruises and that a large clot had formed on her brain, which was the cause of her death. Cecilia's funeral took place on Thursday, 29 June 1899 at Galleywood Church. It was attended by Samuel Crozier, but after the service he was arrested on a charge of manslaughter and taken to the Shire Hall in Chelmsford town centre.

On Friday, 14 July 1899, at the Galleywood School, the coroner's jury returned a verdict of manslaughter, but on the following Friday Crozier appeared before the magistrates at a hearing held at the Shire Hall, where he was informed that the charge had been changed to one of murder.

At the subsequent trial held at Chelmsford Assizes, the jury, after having heard all of the evidence in the case, and after a very brief deliberation, agreed with the charge and returned a verdict of murder. Mr Justice Wills, who was the judge in the case, expressed the opinion that Crozier had been convicted on the 'clearest possible evidence of a cruel murder'.

Crozier's defence was that his wife was a drunk and would often fall over, knocking and hitting herself against the household furniture and falling to the floor. It was also suggested by Crozier's defence that Cecilia had in fact woken on the Sunday morning, only to fall over and strike her head on the inn's bar, but no evidence was provided to support such a theory. A petition, requesting a reprieve of the death sentence which had been passed on Crozier, was rejected by the Home Secretary, who declined to interfere with the decision made at the Assizes.

The story of the murder of Cecilia Jane Crozier threw up some intriguing points. Samuel Crozier had been married before to a Hannah Everitt, a woman with whom he had tied the knot on 29 March 1876. She had remained his wife for twenty-one years until she died on 2 January 1898 in Billericay, reportedly a lunatic. There were, however, no reports of Crozier having been violent towards her throughout the years of their marriage. If this is in fact correct, it begs the question as to why, in such a short period of time, Crozier had become the violent man who had murdered Cecilia.

As is known, theirs was an extremely brief relationship. They had first become romantically involved in the latter part of 1898 and were married in January 1899. Soon after they were married, Cecilia was seen with black eyes and bruises and cuts to her face. When her body was examined after her death, bruising was discovered to different parts of her body.

The explanation for her injuries is quite straightforward. Either she was, as Crozier claimed, a useless drunk, and acquired her injuries through falling over when inebriated, or Crozier was violent towards her. If Crozier was violent, the question is why?

At the time, women were seen as the property of their husbands. Wedding vows included a woman promising to honour and obey her husband, and during the assault by Crozier on Cecilia, which resulted in her death, nobody stepped in to stop the assault from continuing. Sadly, what exacerbated the situation was the possibility that Crozier didn't recognise that he was actually doing anything wrong, and simply believed that the way he was behaving towards his wife was not only acceptable, but his right as a husband.

By 1902 women's rights had still not achieved its aims: political parties made vain promises, and progress was slow. With this in mind, Emmeline Pankhurst, a Labour Party member, quit the National Union and set up the Women's Social and Political Union, along with other disaffected members of the London-based National Union. The main aim of the new group was votes for women on the same basis as men, and members were prepared to achieve their aims by militant means if necessary. The time for talking was over as far as they were concerned. They were convinced that actions and deeds secure more progress than words alone.

Despite the splitting of the organisation, the NUWWS went from strength to strength, and by 1914 it had more than 500 branches up and down the country which equated to some 100,000 members.

The NUWSS had not aligned itself to any one particular political party. Instead it campaigned in support of perspective candidates at a general election who were supportive of women being given the vote. Well, that was their position up until 1912, but the Conciliation Bill of 1911 changed their stance.

The Bill, which was the second of its kind – the first had been the previous year in 1910 – was about trying to extend the right of women to be allowed to vote throughout the United Kingdom and Ireland. It was debated in May 1911 and won a majority of 255 to 88 to go forward as a Private Members Bill, and was promised a week of government time. But, in November 1911, the then Liberal Prime Minister, Herbert Asquith, announced that he was in favour of progressing the Manhood Suffrage Bill instead. Understandably this left a lot of women feeling annoyed, angry and extremely betrayed.

Millicent Fawcett, who herself was a Liberal supporter, felt particularly let down by Asquith and the Liberal Party, who she believed had purposely employed delaying tactics to ensure the Conciliation Bill did not become law. This resulted in the NUWSS playing their own political games and they changed their support to the Labour Party. This wasn't because they had suddenly changed their political bent, but because by supporting labour they put pressure on Asquith and the Liberal Party. For them to progress and cement their own politics in the minds of the British public, they needed the Labour party to remain weak.

The outbreak of the First World War caused a split amongst the ranks of the NUWSS. The majority of its members supported the war, but there was also a small minority who did not. The organisation was very active during the war. They set up an 'employment register'. This involved recording all of the men who had enlisted in the armed forces and the jobs that they had left behind, so that their vacant jobs could then be filled by women who had registered with them looking for work. They also financed women's hospital units that were deployed in France, such as the Scottish Women's Hospitals for Foreign Service, but only employed female doctors and nurses.

After the war, the NUWSS rebranded itself and became the National Union of Societies for Equal Citizenship, under the leadership of its new President, Eleanor Rathbone, with the organisation's new focus being to equalise suffrage. The organisation split in 1928, one of which, the Union of Townswomen's Guilds, which focused on the issues of women's welfare and education, still exists to this day.

Eleanor Rathbone, later went on to become one of the MPs for the Combined English Universities as an independent. A position she held between 30 May 1929 and 2 January 1946, the latter being the date of her death.

What was apparent about all of the women's groups which started life in the mid to late part of the nineteenth century was that the women who were their members were nearly all affluent, well to do individuals who were from well-off families. I am not sure that any of them were women from the working classes who possibly had children and worked in some dirty and dangerous backstreet factory.

I have gone down this particular road as far as I dare, which I believe was necessary, to provide a background to the matter as it was on a national level, but I believe that taking it any further, would risk taking the story away from its original title.

At the forefront of the women's movement was the Women's Liberal Association, and the following pages are filled with information about many of their early meetings, including the names of some of those who were influential in the struggle for women's rights.

There were men in the political arena who supported women's suffrage, some for the right reasons, simply because they realised that the world had changed, and moved forward, and no amount of resistance to women being kept back was how things should be.

Others maybe supported the changes for nothing more than political reasons, as they saw it as an opportunity for acquiring more votes for their Party.

The inaugural meeting of the Chelmsford Women's Liberal Association took place on the evening of Wednesday, 24 July 1889, at the Corn Exchange, Chelmsford. It was chaired by Mr W.W. Duffield, with a relatively large gathering of interested parties also in attendance. Mr Duffield began by speaking about the advantages of having such an association in the town, and how seriously he took political matters, which were worthy of considerable respect. Anything less sent out the message to people that politics were not matters of serious state importance.

One of those present at the meeting was Mr Walter McLaren, the Member of Parliament for Crewe, who officially put forward the proposal to form the Chelmsford Association:

> That this meeting heartily approves of the formation of a Liberal Women's Association in the Chelmsford Division, and believe it will do much to strengthen the Liberal Party: this meeting further condemns the Irish policy of the Government, more especially the imprisonment of Mr Conybeare and the Irish Members of Parliament, who have so bravely stood up for the liberty of the Irish people.

Mr McLaren continued by speaking in favour of women in politics and votes for women, and said that he believed this participation would be achieved before the dissolution of the then Parliament. In any case he believed it was an inevitable event, which would happen sooner than later. Sadly, it would take a good many years, as well as the First World War, for his hopes and dreams to be realised. McLaren made mention of Mr Conybeare, whom he said was a gentleman and deserved the thanks of the nation for the way in which he had braved the imprisonment that he knew awaited him if he went to Ireland to help the poor people of the country. His reason for going there was not to incite anybody to commit crime of any kind. He went to Ireland to show benevolence, and his only offence consisted of relieving the acute distress of some of the evicted tenants. Mr McLaren remarked, 'If only the entire nation would rise up against these proceedings, brought in by the British Government.'

Mrs McLaren seconded her husband's proposal to set up the Chelmsford branch of the Women's Liberal Association, a sentiment for which she was loudly applauded. The motion was carried unanimously. The newly formed Chelmsford branch took the total of these associations nationally to around 100, with a collective membership of 35,000 to 40,000.

Miss Conybeare was the next to speak. She began by expressing her willingness to assist the Association in whatever way she could. She followed this with an extremely interesting account of her experiences in Ireland. She said that the shameful and disgraceful manner in which her brother had been treated would in the end do their cause some good. She could not believe that putting her brother in prison in this way would do Mr Balfour's cause of law and order any good whatsoever. Mr Balfour would go on to become the British prime minister between 1902 and 1905.

She went on to explain the high esteem that the poor people of Ireland appeared to hold her brother in. When he was conveyed by train from Lifford to Derry Gaol, the train was packed with policemen, not to protect him, but to prevent the people from trying to break him free from custody. For some inexplicable reason the authorities wouldn't allow Miss Conybeare to accompany her brother on the train.

Many newspaper articles at the time refer to just 'Miss Conybeare', with no mention of her Christian name, but she was the sister of Charles Augustus Vansittart Conybeare, who had three sisters: Katherine M. Conybeare, who died in 1882, Clara Jane Constance Conybeare, who died in 1888, which left Georgina Emily Conybeare. Strangely enough, she married in October 1888, but she still seems to have been referred to as Miss Conybeare after this time.

A very well attended meeting of the Chelmsford Women's Liberal Association took place on the evening of Thursday, 28 November 1889, at the town's Public Hall, to hear an address by

Miss Conybeare, sister of Mr Charles Conybeare, the Liberal MP for Camborne for ten years between 1885 and 1895.

Miss Conybeare spoke about the Maryborough trials and evictions in Gweedore in Ireland and the effects that had on the families concerned. Mr W.W. Duffield, who again presided over the meeting, was joined on the stage by Miss Conybeare, the Association's President, Mrs Christy, the Honorary Secretary, and Mrs Ambrose Darby, Mrs Munnion and Mrs Impey.

Miss Conybeare made an appeal on behalf of the Women's Liberal Association, in which she said they were hopeful that the Association would spread throughout Chelmsford and in doing so greatly increase its numbers. Another hope was that the rich and poor of the town would join hands and work together for the benefit of each other. Miss Conybeare added that the Women's Liberal Association of Chelmsford wanted to educate the town's women in the political questions of the day, in order that when the time came they might use their influence on the right side of the argument.

By way of example, Miss Conybeare described the trial of Father M'Fadden at Maryborough in Ireland, which in part she had witnessed, and which she said was a travesty of law and justice. She explained how the jury was packed with Protestant men, rather than being a fair split between Catholics and Protestants. The policemen who gave evidence did so by committing acts of gross perjury, which resulted in one man receiving a sentence of ten years' penal servitude, and he wasn't even present in court to defend himself.

It was through such meetings, and such groups as the Women's Liberal Association, that more women were enlightened and educated about the ways of the modern world and how they could influence it in a positive way. They had to guard against allowing themselves being brainwashed into believing that their only value in life was as wives, mothers and homemakers. They needed to embrace education, world affairs and politics, and fight for such issues as the right to vote and equality with men. Many had the desire to do this, but in many cases they didn't have the means: they were tied to a husband who told them what to do, and a family who needed them to be there to look after them. Many were in service so being able to get time off from their work was not easy. For others it was the fear of losing their employment, which in many cases also meant losing a roof over their head, which kept them from becoming active in such groups as the Women's Liberal Association. The people these women worked for, the wealthier individuals in society, would not necessarily look favourably upon such actions. An attitude was deeply imbedded in society that the 'have nots' should know their place and not try to better themselves. The status quo was in the hands of the 'haves', and they were in no rush to share what they had.

The Public Hall at Moulsham on Thursday, 12 December 1889 was the venue for a meeting of the Chelmsford Women's Liberal Association, to hear an address by Doctor Kate Mitchell on the subject of 'Women's work and temperance'. The Reverend J.M. Whiteman, who chaired the meeting, said that he was very happy at the assistance women were giving to the cause of temperance. Doctor Mitchell began by congratulating Miss Conybeare on forming a branch of the Women's Liberal Association in Chelmsford, adding that with most of the counties surrounding London being Tory run, she hoped that these associations would flourish over time with more and more of them being formed. She also felt the need to vindicate her position as an orator on women's rights, by clarifying that she felt it was acceptable for women to have a public life as well as a private one, but for those who chose to venture in to the public world, their motives for doing so should be for the right reasons and not be connected to reasons of personal vanity. This was the very reason why she did not approve of the women who were associated with the Primrose League, which was an organisation founded to spread Conservative principles.

Doctor Mitchell continued her speech, highlighting the various branches of work that had been opened up to women, and adding that if the British Women's Temperance Association entered into politics more than they had done so previously, and if the Women's Liberal Association made temperance one of their main aims, then she believed that acts of drunkenness would rapidly be greatly reduced.

Miss Conybeare thanked Doctor Mitchell for her kind and supportive words. She was keen to inform her audience about the children of Hoxton, who were given packets of sweets at public houses as a means of enticing them in to the premises. She was also of the view that all public houses should be shut on a Sunday, as was the case with all other places of public amusement, thus keeping the day free for such family pastimes as going to church.

The Women's Liberal Association held a meeting at the Co-operative Stores' Assembly Room on the evening of Monday, 11 December 1893, but unfortunately there was a very poor turn out, suggesting either that the Association was not a flourishing enterprise, or that there wasn't much interest in the political points that were up for discussion. The Association's President, Miss Conybeare, provided an alternative explanation for the poor attendance, saying that Chelmsford women were otherwise engaged in view of the fact that Christmas was fast approaching.

Miss Seel gave a speech on the topic of 'What women have to do with politics', which was well received. Miss Phillips presented the Association's annual report, which besides other things showed that there had been an increase in membership, which for the Chelmsford branch meant they had 115 members.

On Thursday, 6 September 1894 a fairly well-attended meeting took place at the Crane Court Assembly Room, Chelmsford, of the Chelmsford Women's Liberal Association. The meeting was chaired by the Reverend F.W. Atkin, who told those present that the Parish Councils Act would bring them closer to getting allotments, public libraries and piped water supplies for people's homes. The new Act would also allow them to deal with what would universally be described as 'unhealthy dwellings'.

Miss Conybeare addressed the meeting, enumerating the principal measures that had been passed by the present Liberal government. She said that the Women's Liberal Federation was a great power throughout the country, and that the Parish Councils Act came with benefits for the common man and woman, which she hoped would result in women being allowed to be part of Parish and District Councils. Some of the male speakers, although not necessarily against the inclusion of women councillors, didn't see such a progression happening with any particular immediacy.

The Women's Liberal Federation had only been formed in 1886 from an amalgamation of fifteen local Women's Liberal Associations. By 1904 this had risen to 494 affiliated associations, with a combined membership of just under 68,000. One of their main objectives was to promote just legislation for women through the introduction of them being able to vote at both local and parliamentary elections.

In the 1901 census there are numerous Conybeares living in the Chelmsford area, and there is more than one family with that surname living in Moulsham Street in the town, but in 1891 there was only one such family with that surname shown as living in Chelmsford. The 1891 census records that Harry (43), a retired army pensioner, and Lilie Conybeare (33), and their three daughters, Lilie, Ethel and Minnie, were residing at 59 Moulsham Street, Chelmsford, where they lodged with widow Mrs Marzena Maples.

A search of the marriage records shows that Harry Conybeare married Vivian Eleanore Lilian Latitia D'Vain on 8 October 1881 in Aldershot, when she was 23 years of age. This appears to be the same woman who is shown on the 1891 census, but instead of using the name on her wedding certificate, she is simply referred to as Lilie. She also appears to be the same woman who was the leader of the Chelmsford branch of the Women's Liberal Federation, and who spoke at the meeting in Chelmsford on Thursday 6 September 1894.

Tuesday, 10 March 1896 saw a very well-attended meeting take place in the Ball Room at the Shire Hall in Chelmsford, in connection with the Chelmsford Women's Total Abstinence Union. The main speaker for the evening was Mr W.S. Caine, a well-known temperance advocate. He had been due to attend along with his wife, who due to illness had been unable to accompany her husband. Also present, besides others, were Mrs Marriage, Mrs Morton, Mrs Pash, Miss Copland and Miss E. Impey, the Union's Honorary Secretary.

Miss Copland read out the annual report, which covered such areas as membership. It was regretted that during the previous year membership had not increased as had been forecast. The Society had a total of 392 members, with 65 having joined throughout the year, and new branches had also been formed at nearby Felsted and Braintree.

There was much discussion at the meeting about the English Sunday Closing Bill, which was due to have its second reading in the House of Commons on 6 May that year. Those present were requested to urge their particular Member of Parliament to support the Bill, regardless of their political persuasion. It was also agreed that a petition from the Society would be forwarded to Parliament requesting it to stop the sale of intoxicating liquor on Sundays.

A copy of the petition was also sent to the Prime Minister, Lord Salisbury, the Leader of the House of Commons, Mr Balfour, the Secretary of State for the Home Department, Sir M.W. Ridley, and the MP for Chelmsford, Mr Thomas Usborne. One of those present at the meeting, Mr Reeve, stated that he had previously sent a similar petition to Mr Usborne, who reluctantly presented it in the House.

Mr Caine, speaking in respect of the Sunday Closing Bill, pointed out that there were different issues, which, if the Bill was eventually passed, would be addressed. As he saw it, ensuring families spent time together on the Sabbath was important as it ensured that, besides other things, they could attend church together, but it wasn't just about stopping men spending all their time, and money, in the pub; it also ensured that people who worked in the drinks industry had one day off so that they too could spend time with their families. This was of course at a time when a working day was quite often much longer than eight hours, and where lunch breaks were not a right.

Mr Caine suggested that there were abundant social and economic reasons to encourage the members of the Chelmsford Women's Total Abstinence Union to agitate for Sunday closing. The drinking habits of a large percentage of the nation's men were not only damaging to the very fabric of family life, but also to the country's economy, as many men missed work due to being drunk or suffering from hangovers. Families, particularly young children, often went without a substantial meal due to their fathers spending their wages in drinking houses, and the long-term health of these same men who were the heavy drinkers, was put at risk. As Mr Caine saw it, the only sensible remedy was a total abstinence for individuals, and an officially sanctioned introduction of prohibition by the British government. He also made reference to what was known as the Gothenburg System, a scheme which had been brought in to reduce drunkenness in Sweden, but which had proved not to be as effective as everybody claimed it was, as about five times as many people had been arrested for drunkenness in Gothenburg as had in Liverpool. In essence it was an attempt to control the consumption of alcohol. He also touched on the Local Veto Bill, which Mr Caine said was a reasonable measure, and in line with a system of self-government for local communities, which he believed would result in many towns up and down the country suppressing the sale of liquor in their own communities, which he believed was a reasonable power for them to have.

It was quite clear from such meetings, and the groups which held them, that the woes of society were blamed on the excessive consumption of alcohol. It appears that the majority of those who consumed alcohol were men. Women who were acquainted with drinking establishments were either barmaids or women of the night. Few were able to just have one pint of beer, one glass of wine, or a single measure of scotch. In many cases they would carry on drinking until they were comatose, as if by doing so they could blot out their constant struggle with everyday life. Those who suffered most from the ravages of the demon drink were the wives and children, to whom the inebriated men would return once they had spent their money. This explains the zeal with which women fought against the sale and consumption of alcohol: they were fed up with seeing their husband's wages, which could be better spent buying food and clothes for the family, swilling around in the bottom of a glass. With more than forty public houses dotted throughout the Chelmsford area, ready and waiting to quench a man's thirst and separate him from his hard-earned money, it was no easy task.

Large provincial towns such as Chelmsford saw an increase in the number of large, purpose-built public houses in the town during the mid to late 1800s. With the coming of the railways, a number of hotels were built very close to the stations, catering for the tired and weary passengers on their arrival in the town.

A well-attended meeting of the Chelmsford Women's Liberal Association took place at the Corn Exchange on the evening of Thursday, 19 March 1896. The meeting was chaired by Mr W.B. Duffield, the son of Alderman W.W. Duffield. In what turned out to be a lively debate, and one that was certainly devoid of large numbers of women, the chairman, in his address, referred to the country as being unpopular on the international stage. He said that the Conservative Prime Minister, Robert Cecil, Marquess of Salisbury, appeared to have three mottos in his dealings with other nations. The first was to brag and bluster, the next was to apologise and explain, and the third was surrender.

The reporting of the meeting highlighted the inequality between men and women. Although this was a meeting of the Chelmsford Women's Liberal Association, the press reporting included detailed content of the addresses made by Mr Duffield and Mr Bertram, yet dismissed women's contribution with the brief and condescending snippet 'Countess Alice Kearney followed with one of her interesting addresses'. How this meeting was supposed to assist the cause of women in society, at either a national or local level, is hard to fathom. The content appears to have been totally devoid of anything to do with women and their right to be able to vote in elections, or achieve equality with men.

On Tuesday, 3 December 1907 a meeting took place at the Shire Hall in Chelmsford, which was addressed by Lord Tweedmouth, who at the time was the First Lord of the Admiralty. Not surprisingly, his speech in the main was in relation to naval policy. Several of the suffragettes managed to acquire tickets to gain entry to the Shire Hall so as to attend the meeting. It was only a matter of minutes into Lord Tweedmouth's speech when several of the women stood up to interrupt him, but they were almost immediately ejected from the premises. During the efforts to have the suffragettes removed from the building, some damage was caused to the inside of the premises, indicating that they did not go quietly or willingly. Lord Tweedmouth was quick to comment that such conduct as had been witnessed that evening showed that those who demanded suffrage for women were not fit to exercise it.

After their ejection, the suffragettes held their own meeting outside the building, where Mrs Flora Drummond, one of the suffragette leaders, addressed a large crowd that had gathered.

At the end of the meeting Lord Tweedmouth made the short journey along Duke Street to Chelmsford railway station, where a group of the suffragettes surrounded him. Although not physically violent towards him, they bombarded him with question after question. Lord Tweedmouth asked them to have patience, and then, somewhat in contradiction of his stance during the meeting, told the women that he had been prepared to argue with them in the meeting at the Shire Hall. On hearing this, Flora Drummond replied, 'My dear, you are not brave enough. We want brave men for our cause.'

Lord Tweedmouth replied that he would be prepared to give women the vote when it was decided that they should sit in the Houses of Parliament. Flora Drummond and her female followers responded by letting Lord Tweedmouth know that they would be prepared to heckle the Tory Party if they came to power, just like they had with the Liberal Party.

What the people of Chelmsford, especially the women, made of the evening's events is not known, but it would be a fair guess that they would have been somewhat shocked at what they witnessed. In the main, this was not the way women behaved or were expected to conduct themselves.

Grace Chappelow was born in Islington, London, on 3 February 1884, and by 1910 she was living in the hamlet of Nounsley, near Hatfield Peverel, which oddly enough has a Chelmsford postmark, but is in the parliamentary constituency of Braintree. She is connected to Chelmsford through visits to the town and was a committed suffragette in the early years of the twentieth century. She became a member of the Women's Social and Political Union and was so dedicated to the cause that she ended up spending time as a prisoner in Holloway Prison for smashing windows. Where, why and how she acquired her strong views on women's suffrage is not clear. Her father was a chartered accountant, and his wage helped provide a fairly wealthy standard of living for him and his family. Grace attended the North London Collegiate School, which was, and still is, an independent day school for girls, formerly known as Queen's College.

When Grace was one of its pupils, the school was situated in Camden Town, but in 1940 the school moved to a much larger premises in Edgware, Middlesex. The headmistress during Grace's time as a pupil was Dr Sophie Bryant, whose CV was outstanding given the limited educational opportunities available to women at that time. She became one of the first women to obtain a first-class Honours degree in Mental and Moral Sciences. She later obtained a degree in Mathematics, both qualifications coming from the University of London, which had first allowed women to take degree courses in 1878. In 1884 she obtained a further degree, this time a Doctor of Science. She had educational books published on the topic of geometry. She was one of the first women to be appointed to sit on a Royal Committee, when in 1894 and 1895 she was part of the Bryce Commission on Secondary Education. All of these things she had achieved before becoming the headmistress of the North London Collegiate in 1895.

If ever a young woman needed a positive female role model to follow in life, they could have done a lot worse than to aspire to follow in the footsteps of Sophie Bryant. Maybe it was she who started Grace on her path to supporting the campaign for women's suffrage.

In about 1901, when Grace was just 17 years of age, her father, John Stephen Chappelow, moved out of the family home. By the time of the 1911 census he was living at Marlcliff House, Ethel Road, St Peter's, Isle of Thanet, Kent. It was definitely a permanent arrangement as although he was recorded as being married, he had two servants and a single female visitor staying with him.

The well-known suffragettes Sylvia Pankhurst, Flora Drummond and Helen Ogston, visited the Corn Exchange at Chelmsford on

19 November 1908, where Pankhurst and Drummond both made speeches. The reason for their visit to the town was the upcoming Mid Essex by-election. It was not common practice for women to give such speeches at the time, that had always been the sole domain of men. Whether it was because of what they were saying, or due to the fact that they were women, they were not well received, and matters quickly went from bad to worse when the crowd turned on them. It started with heckling and verbal abuse and resulted in the women being physically accosted by some of the rowdy crowd who they were trying to address.

The following evening they tried again to make their voices heard. The town centre was absolutely packed solid with people, so great was the anticipation that the streets literarily came to a standstill. The ladies had learnt their lesson from the previous evening, so rather than address the assembled crowd outdoors whilst stood on a flimsy platform, Flora Drummond chose to speak from the comparative safety of an upstairs window at the town's Bell Hotel.

On 27 November 1908 there were two meetings which took place in Chelmsford. One at the Shire Hall, which is situated at the very top of the High Street, and the other at the Marconi Building, situated about a mile north of the High Street. The meeting at the Shire Hall was led by the Women's Freedom League and the one at the Marconi Building was for the National Union of Women's Suffrage. I have to say that it is not known whether or not Grace Chappelow actually attended any of the Chelmsford meetings, but it just goes to show the level of feelings there were in the town about the topic of women's suffrage. Considering the reaction to the first meeting which took place in Chelmsford on 19 November 1908, it wasn't entirely supportive.

Grace Chappelow was certainly a character, someone who had strong views on the subject of women's suffrage, a topic that she was clearly passionate about. By 1909 she had joined the Women's Social and Political Union (WSPU), which had been founded on 10 October 1903, by Emmeline and Christabel Pankhurst. The organisation's motto included the phrase, 'deeds not words', and was the leading militant organisation campaigning for women's suffrage in the United Kingdom.

The members engaged in a number of different tactics in an effort to get their views and opinions across to both politicians and the general public. They attended meetings where it was known politicians would be speaking and heckled them or shouted them down. They held marches and demonstrations and set fire to post boxes, they smashed the windows of prominent buildings and carried out night-time arson attacks on unoccupied houses and churches. When they received custodial sentences they often went on hunger strike, which led to force feeding to avoid their early release.

Chappelow ardently embraced the WSPU's motto of 'deeds not words'. In September 1909, she was arrested and spent five days in jail for disrupting a meeting at the Palace Theatre in Leicester where the then Home Secretary, Winston Churchill, was speaking. In November 1910, when she was living at Nounsley, Hatfield Peverel, she was, along with 119 other suffragettes, involved in planning a raid on the House of Commons but this did not result in any of the women being prosecuted. In 1911, she was arrested for an attempted raid on the House of Commons.

In March 1912, a number of meetings were held at the Shire Hall in Chelmsford in relation to women's suffrage, one of which she spoke at; the topic of her speech was the growth of the suffrage movement.

Later that year she was arrested for smashing windows at Mansion House, the Lord Mayor of London's official residence. Along with three other suffragettes, she was sentenced to two months with hard labour at Holloway Prison in London. On her release, she smuggled out a cup and a knife, one assumes as souvenirs of her incarceration. Both of these items are now on display at the Chelmsford Museum. The mug was subsequently engraved, presumably by Chappelow with the words, 'Down with Asquith Nov 1918, Give Women Votes …. Be Free.'

Soon after her release from Holloway, she was in trouble once again. This time she was arrested by Witham Police when her dog attacked and bit a political agent. She subsequently appeared at the local police court, where she was found guilty in relation to a 'dangerous dog' offence and fined 14 shillings, which she refused to pay. She was sent to Chelmsford prison for fourteen days.

Grace Chappelow certainly did her bit to further women's suffrage as an active campaigner and even received a certificate, signed by Emmeline Pankhurst, in acknowledgement of this and her time spent in prison.

Whilst the suffragettes had been fighting their battle for the furtherance of women, an act of Parliament had come into being which most definitely helped their cause, but did not appear to have been given great prominence in the national newspapers.

The Qualification of Women (County and Borough Councils) Act 1907, came in to being and outlined the rights of certain women, who were also rate payers, to be elected to either Borough or County Councils throughout England and Wales. In previous times when women had attempted to stand for such places on the London County Council, this was challenged in the courts by certain individuals who could not comprehend a woman holding such a position. This was a time when the only women who could apply for such a role would have been single. A married woman would in most cases only be allowed one opinion, that of her husband.

Women had been allowed to sit on the newly formed Urban and Rural District Councils since 1894 and had also sat on boards that dealt with the Poor Law Act and the 1870 Education Act. However, despite these advancements for women they were still met with a certain amount of resistance, as many men still thought that a woman's place was in the home as a wife and mother, or if they did work, that it should be in a factory, hospital, or shop; and they should most definitely not have an opinion of their own.

The 1907 Act was a move in the right direction for women's rights as it also provided widows and unmarried women the right to stand for election. As a result of the changes, five women were elected to their Borough or County Councils, but sadly none of them were from Chelmsford.

Although there were numerous women's-suffrage-related meetings which took place in Chelmsford town centre, the only individual from the district who I have been able to find, who was a noted active campaigner for women's rights, was Grace Chappelow. It is inconceivable that there was no strong local suffragette movement in Chelmsford, but any information about that movement and the women who were members of it has evaded me.

There were others from nearby Essex towns, such as the Lock sisters from Ingatestone, Kitty Marion who was raised in Great Dunmow and another Eliza Vaughan from Rayne, near Braintree.

CHAPTER THREE

Employment

Chelmsford, like most locations, has seen its population steadily increase in size over the years. Although now officially a City, having acquired that status on 1 June 2012 as part of the Queen's Diamond Jubilee celebrations, I will refer to it amongst these pages as a town, as that is what it was during the time frame that this book covers.

I have looked at the work carried out by women over the sixty years between 1851 and 1911 using census records. In keeping with the area having been a fairly affluent one, there are many examples of large family homes from that time still in existence. Having said that, it will come as no shock to learn that the employment which most working women found themselves engaged in was that of domestic service. For some that meant living in, whilst others travelled to and from their place of work on a daily basis.

The other listed employment for women, according to the different censuses and repeated here in no particular order, included nurses, teachers, cooks, and weavers. It has to be remembered that for most of this time, it would have been mainly single women who made up the town's female workforce.

During the latter part of the nineteenth century and the beginning of the twentieth, and particularly before the outbreak of the First World War, life for a woman was in effect mapped out for her from the moment she was born. As soon as she was old enough to work and bring money in to the family home, she did, but once she was married, her responsibilities changed. She was then expected to stay at home to have and look after her husband's children. She had to keep the home clean and tidy, and look after her husband, with all that that involved.

One of Chelmsford's biggest factory employers was Marconi's, which first opened for business in Hall Street in December 1898, after the Marconi's 'Wireless Telegraph and Signal Company' was formed on 20 July 1897. The company had acquired a British patent to produce wireless's in March of that year. Just three years after it opened, the company name was changed to 'Marconi's Wireless Telegraph Company' but other than that it was business as usual.

As an aside, and unrelated to women, 14 April 1912 saw the sinking of the *Titanic*. The connection between the sinking and Marconi was the ship's radio operators. These men were not members of the ship's crew, they were employees of the Marconi's Wireless Telegraph Company, with their primary responsibility being to send messages for the passengers. There were two radio operators on board the *Titanic*, junior wireless operator, Harold Sydney Bride, and senior wireless operator, John George Phillips, who was known as 'Jack'.

In June 1912, Marconi's work load having greatly increased, and in need of bigger premises, the company moved from its original Hall Street location to a brand new, purpose built site at New Street, Chelmsford. Marconi more than proved its worth during the First World War, by making equipment that allowed instant communication between units who were on different parts of the battlefield. A Marconi employee came up with a technique which allowed the Allies to be able to locate enemy positions on either land or at sea, by pinpointing their position when they transmitted wireless messages. This technique was used to great effect during the Battle of Jutland, when the Imperial German Fleet left their base in Germany. The Royal Navy were informed, and were then able to send their own ships in to the area of the North Sea and confront the Germans before they could get anywhere near the British coast.

Marconi also employed women at their works, and photographs exist of them working at the Chelmsford site around 1902, but what they did, how many worked there and when, is not known.

Close to Marconi's new works at New Street, was the already well-established Hoffmann Manufacturing Company. Not only did they employ women, but they also produced much needed ball bearings for the war effort. In September 1917 the company was nationalised by the Ministry of Munitions for the remainder of the war.

I have included the other aspects of the work women undertook during the First World War in Chapter Four. The censuses covering the period between 1851 and 1911 give a valuable insight into the population of Chelmsford and the role women played in the life of the town, especially in providing a detailed breakdown of employment. By examining the differences in each decade we can see how things changed across a sixty-year period.

1851

The population of Chelmsford in 1851 stood at 7,889. Remarkably, 4,151, or nearly 60 per cent, of these were female, and of these 1,098, or just over 26 per cent, were married. Of those who worked, 491 were servants and 13 were nurses, 12 of whom were working for individual families. There were also six who were employed as teachers and one who was working as a cook. There were no women working as either weavers or factory workers.

Most large towns had what was known as a Union Workhouse. This was an establishment run by the local authority, which housed members of the local population who were homeless and had no other family members to support them. Although the origins of the workhouse system can be traced back to the Poor Law Act of 1388, the workhouses that sprung up at the end of the eighteenth and the beginning of the nineteenth century came under the control of the New Poor Law of 1834.

Today's welfare state looks after the population. While they are of working age, those who are unemployed or who are unable to work because of illness or disease, are paid a financial benefit so that they can afford to live and eat. For some this is a short-term scenario, while for others it lasts their entire adult life. Part of the welfare state also allows elderly people who have reached retirement age, and no longer work, a pension which covers their living costs including their accommodation.

During the second half of the nineteenth century and up until the birth of the welfare state in 1906, when the Liberal Party brought in welfare reforms, there was no such thing as a pension. The bottom line was no job, no money, and for the people who found themselves in that situation, that meant not being able to pay the rent, as very few people were wealthy enough to own their own property. It also meant not being able to feed themselves adequately.

The welfare state brought in pensions for all those who were aged seventy and above in 1908, and three years later the National Insurance Act 1911 brought in free medical treatment and sick pay of ten shillings per week for a period of 26 weeks.

For 1851, records show that the Chelmsford Union Workhouse, which was in Wood Street, and had first opened its doors in 1837, had a population of 329, of which 127 were women.

1861

Amazingly not much had changed population wise in Chelmsford in the ten years between 1851 and 1861. The overall population had actually fallen by 82 people to 7,807. The number of these who were women had fallen by 10 to 4,141 and of these 1,190 were married, which was an increase of 120, meaning percentage-wise there had been very little shift in the figures. Some 426 women were recorded as having been employed as servants, and 6 were working as nurses. There were no women recorded as being employed as teachers, weavers or factory workers, but twenty-six were working as cooks, which was a massive increase on the previous census.

In relation to employment I do not suggest that these were the only jobs undertaken by women. The reason for choosing teacher, servant, nurse, weaver, factory worker and cook as jobs to quote figures for, is because they were good examples of the type of work that women were able to get.

By 1861 the population of the workhouse in Wood Street had shrunk to 254, with 111 of the inmates being women. This was a premises which had been built to cater for 400 people, such was the expected demand.

1871

The number of people living in Chelmsford according to the 1871 census was 9,292, an increase of 1,499. This was just as much about an increase in births as it was about people moving in to the town to live and work. Of these, 4,877 were women, an increase of 736 on the figures from the previous census, which is roughly an 18 per cent rise. The number of married women had increased by 206 to 1,396, which was a rise of about 17 per cent.

Work-wise only three Chelmsford women were recorded as being employed as teachers, none of whom had been born in the town. Servants had risen to 490, which was nearly back to the level of 1851, while 20 were shown as cooks. There were eleven women employed as nurses, and there was no record of any women being employed as weavers or factory workers, although the latter two occupations were sometimes included in the same category.

The figures for 1871 show that there was not much change in the numbers of inmates who were resident at the Chelmsford Union Workhouse. There were a total of 278, of whom 110 were female.

1881

Chelmsford's population had increased in size by a relatively small number of people by 1881. The new figure was 10,035, which meant that in ten years it had risen by just 742.

The number of women had increased by 1,473 to 5,340, of whom 1,497 were married women. The number of them who were teachers had drastically increased to 29, while the number working as servants had also increased to a massive 602. There were 86 women working as cooks, 74 employed as nurses, 52 factory workers and 2 weavers.

The population of the workhouse was 255, with only 76 of the inmates being female. This was the lowest number of women resident at the workhouse between 1851 and 1911. In 1886 the workhouse in Wood Street was totally destroyed by fire, so the authorities set about rebuilding a new premises on the same site, which opened in 1889 with enough beds to cater for 435 inmates.

1891

The population of Chelmsford in 1891 was 11,037, an increase of 1,002 from the previous census. Of these 5,811 were women, which was an increase of just under 500, and of these, 1,628 were married women. The number working as servants had dropped by 80 to 502. There were no women recorded as being employed as teachers, and only 2 were cooks. Eight women were nurses, and there were no women recorded working as either weavers or factory workers.

A snapshot of the figures for 1881 and 1891 shows that although there is an increase of 502 women, the number of those shown as working has dropped drastically from 872 to 532.

The figures for the workhouse this time round were very similar to those of 1881. There were a total of 255 inmates, of which only 76 were women.

1901

The first census of the twentieth century shows the population of Chelmsford had yet again increased, in line with national trends. The new figure was 12,587, which meant that in ten years since the previous census the town's population had increased by just over 2,500. There were 6,464 women, of whom 1,974 were married. Those employed as servants had increased slightly to 535. There were no female teachers. Those working as nurses stood at just 6. Those working as cooks, numbered just 3. There were no female weavers, nor were there any women recorded as working in factories.

This year saw a workhouse population totalling 297, with 82 of them being females.

1911

The 1911 census saw a marked increase in the population of Chelmsford, which had by then risen to 18,021, but which was still just over double the size it had been fifty years earlier in 1861.

Just over half the population, 9,065, were women, and of these 3,055 were married. As the population of the town grew, so did the number of jobs that were available. There were 777 women employed as servants working in homes throughout Chelmsford, suggesting a degree of affluence in the area. There were 105 women employed as cooks, and a further 73 who were working as teachers. Meanwhile, 102 women were working as nurses, and 19 worked in factories. There were no women working as weavers.

The workhouse's inmate population in 1911 was 323, with 139 of those being women.

The combined figures for working women, taken from the job descriptions I have included, amounted to 971, which was the highest number of women in employment in Chelmsford in the sixty years from 1851.

There were other forms of employment for women, with many working with their husbands in such areas as farming and baking. However, they were listed as 'wife' on the census.

It is worth giving this period of time some context. The Industrial Revolution had taken place between about 1760 and 1840, which had ushered in many new jobs in mechanised industries such as cotton spinning. The downside was economic depression, due in part to a reduction in the number of workers needed to do the work, and an over-abundance of manufactured products that were produced by the much-improved machinery.

By 1870 there had been a change in the nation's fortunes, with a period of rapid economic growth, due in part to a second Industrial Revolution, which had begun around 1850.

Workhouses, or local institutions for those who were destitute and poor, could once be found in most villages and towns. In 1777 there were twelve separate parish workhouses in the Chelmsford district, but only three of them could cater for substantial numbers. The institutions at Chelmsford, Great Waltham and Writtle could all officially cater for 100 patients, paupers or inmates, as they were variously known.

The Poor Law Amendment Act 1834 helped formalise how members of local communities would be treated if they fell on hard times and were unable to financially support themselves and their families. The Act transferred the responsibility for looking after the poor to Boards of Guardians, removing it from individual parishes, which in Chelmsford and its surrounding areas, numbered some 35 in total. In essence the Board of Guardians oversaw the work carried out by the Chelmsford Poor Law Union, which was formed on Monday, 10 August 1835.

In 1872 the Public Health Act was enacted. This created urban and rural sanitary authorities, with the workhouses' Boards of Governors being designated as the rural sanitary authority for the parts of the Chelmsford Poor Law Union that did not come under an urban sanitary authority. This system would remain in place for a further fifty-six years, before it was subsequently replaced by the Local Government Act 1929.

The Chelmsford Union Workhouse opened at 48 Wood Street, Moulsham, Chelmsford, in 1837 and could officially cater for a combination of up to 400 men and women. It was almost totally destroyed by fire in 1886, before being rebuilt on the same site, a project which took three years to complete. It reopened in 1889. The new workhouse rose like a phoenix from the ashes, and could cater for thirty-five additional inmates.

I thought it would be interesting to take a brief look at the numbers of inmates of the Chelmsford Union Workhouse between 1851 and 1911, to compare the numbers of men and women.

Year	Women	Men
1851	127	184
1861	111	143
1871	110	169
1881	76	179
1891	82	176
1901	114	184
1911	139	184

As can be seen from the above figures, the numbers of male residents remained reasonably static over the period, while the number of female residents dipped over the first thirty years of the workhouse's existence, before following an upward trend over the course of the next forty years.

Women and children found themselves ensconced in the Chelmsford workhouse through no fault of their own. Lone children might be orphaned, or have been abandoned by their parents, like the Barrott sisters, Emma, Caroline, and Charlotte, who are included on the inmates list at the Chelmsford workhouse on the 1871 census. Similarly, Maria Avis, and her three young children, Ellen, Ann and Elizabeth, found themselves inmates because they were no longer able to financially support themselves.

Throughout November and December 1887 a number of attacks against women took place on the streets of Chelmsford. Each was more violent than the one before.

At the end of November 1887, local resident Mr Walter Cowell, of Broomfield Road, Chelmsford, wrote a letter to a local newspaper warning of the danger to women of being out on their own late at night, especially during the dark, cold winter months. To evidence the comments he made in his letter, he explained that his own wife had been attacked not far from their home in Broomfield Road just before ten o'clock in the evening. Despite a constable being specifically allocated to patrol in and around the area of Broomfield Road and the surrounding streets, another attack took place on Tuesday,13 December 1887.

Miss Clara Smith was employed as an assistant at Mr Bond's drapery shop. Having finished her work she made the short journey on foot back to her lodgings at 1 Rail Villas, Fairfield Road. When she was opposite the surgery of Mr E.H. Carter, she noticed a well-dressed man cross over the road. He continued into Fairfield Road and then walked up the steps leading to Mr Carter's surgery, as if he had arrived for an appointment. A few moments later she realised that the same man was following her, and before she realised what was happening, she felt an arm encircle her waist before she was violently assaulted. Thankfully, and despite the dire predicament she found herself in, she still had the presence of mind to scream out. In doing so she unnerved her assailant, and he made good his escape, leaving her lying on the pavement. She quickly picked herself up and hastily made her way back to her lodgings. On arrival, with her dress covered in mud, she was understandably in a very agitated state, crying uncontrollably and almost becoming hysterical.

Mrs Saltmarsh, who was Miss Smith's landlady, quickly went to fetch PC Cudmore, who lived in Duke Street, almost opposite where the attack had taken place. Constable Cudmore was unable to elicit a detailed description from Miss Smith of what the man who had attacked her looked like or what he was wearing, due to a combination of the darkness and the manner in which she was attacked. She was able to say that he was wearing a long dark overcoat and was carrying an umbrella. After completing his interview, PC Cudmore immediately set off to make enquiries at the numerous public houses that were situated in the vicinity, but to no avail.

Mr Carter was able to confirm that nobody had called at his premises at the time stated. Constable Cudmore did manage to find two women, assistants at a nearby shop, and who also lived in Fairfield Road, who were walking in the same direction as Miss Smith and slightly ahead of her when they heard screams. Sadly, although maybe understandably, they did not go to the woman's assistance or try to establish what had taken place.

Whether the attacker was ever caught, or how many other similar attacks he had carried out, is unknown. One thing is certain though, at the time of telling this story, some 130 years after Miss Smith was attacked, the principle of a woman being out on her own late at night is still not something most sensible people would accept as being the correct course of action, no matter how much of a reflection that is on society. Even with vehicular traffic passing through most streets day and night, CCTV coverage now widespread throughout most towns and cities, street lighting in almost every road in the country, it is still not 100 per cent safe for women on their own to be out late at night, regardless of whether it should or shouldn't be. The situation is made even worse in such circumstances because of mobile phones. Although they are a quick way to call for help should it be needed, people become so engrossed in them that quite often they are not paying attention. Add to this headphones and ear pieces that are so frequently used in unison with the phone, and if anything the danger of a female walking alone during the hours of darkness, is as dangerous now as it was at the time of the attack on Miss Smith, all those years ago.

As far as employment was concerned, did the First World War improve women's lives throughout Great Britain? I for one, believe that it did, an opinion which I will expand upon later. It is a fact that in July 1914, the number of women who were in full-time employment stood at 24 per cent. By the end of the war in November 1918, that figure had risen to 37 per cent. This increase came about purely and simply because of the war; some 2 million women, who hadn't previously been full-time workers now did their bit for their King and country by taking up the work of the men who had relinquished their jobs to go and fight in the war.

Now back to my personal opinion on the subject. The war gave women a freedom which they had never known before. Many of them were in full-time employment for the first time, whilst also carrying out some kind of voluntary work. With their work came an independence that they had never known before, along with a wage which was their own money, an aspect of life that most, if not all of them, would have had absolutely no previous experience. On the matter of wages, in most cases the women would have been reasonably happy with what they were earning, even though it was still less than men had been paid to carry out the exact same work. This was a fact that made the employers extremely happy, and one that encouraged them to want to employ even more women.

It is hard to argue against the fact that the war made a much wider range of jobs available to women, roles that previously would have been deemed too unladylike for them to undertake, especially manual work. It should be remembered that before the war, a secretary was a job predominantly carried out by a man. I would hazard a guess that in today's workplace there are few jobs available for male secretaries, but go back 100 years and it would have been commonplace.

An example of the reverse of the above scenario could clearly be shown when it came to domestic service, which was the same both locally in the Chelmsford area and across the country on a national level. There were, as I see it, three reasons for this. Firstly, in the years immediately following the end of the First World War, people, women especially, expected more out of life in general, because of the high price the war had exacted on them collectively. The lower classes in particular had lost so many of their men folk, which had changed the lives for so many of their families, they simply were not prepared to return to how life was before the war, where many of them were in effect serfs to the upper classes, who had dominated their lives. Secondly, working women now had a much wider choice of jobs available to them. By way of example, clerical work and all that it entailed was an attractive proposition, the pay was better and the working conditions were generally better. Thirdly, besides domestic service having lost much of its appeal to the working women, the middle and upper classes who had previously employed them no longer required so many staff, due to the rise in domestic appliances coming on to the market. Electric kettles had been around since the 1890s, and improved greatly over the course of the following thirty years, so much so, that by 1922 the type that are in abundance today first became available, having been designed by a man called Leslie Large, who worked for Bulpitt & Sons of Birmingham. Other appliances such as gas cookers, came about in around 1922, followed by electric ones round about 1930. The first motorised vacuum cleaner went on sale in America in 1898.

So there you have it. Women's working lives did improve for the better as a result of the First World War, but it wasn't the only factor which determined this statement. With the large number of affluent homes that are dotted around Chelmsford, these same factors certainly had an effect on the town's working women.

What had not changed, however, were women's wages. Women were still paid less than men for doing the same work, and in some cases men were paid twice as much.

There was another, rarely spoken about, matter which was also relevant and certainly worth mentioning. Unions had not always been that supportive of female workers and during the First World War, and in its immediate aftermath, they were downright anti-feminist, possibly because they had one eye on the future. The work that women contributed during the war was a huge boost to the nation's war effort, especially in a town like Chelmsford where the importance of some employers, such as Marconi and Hoffmanns, could not be ignored. But when the war ended the unions wanted the men to get their jobs back, at the expense of the women who had replaced them. Some employers didn't want that as they were making more money by paying the women lower wages than they would have to pay the men. It was an extremely difficult situation. Men who had returned from the war, having answered the call of their King in the nation's time of need, felt that they should be given their old jobs back and that the women who had replaced them should step aside and return to being housewives. With high unemployment, feelings were at fever pitch, the returning married soldiers automatically assumed that their wives would relinquish their jobs and go back to looking after the home.

There was a social stigma attached to this because this was a time when it was seen to be the role of the man to go out to work, be the breadwinner, and provide for his family; sending your wife out to work was not seen as the manly thing to do. I remember when I started secondary school in 1970 – over 50 years later – and my mother got a job as a cook at the same school. My father was not happy, and it caused many rows between them. During one particular argument they had, my dad said to my mum, 'How do you think this makes me look in the eyes of my colleagues?' I remember days of silence between them and dad even took to eating his meals on his own for a while. A bad case of stubbornness if ever there was one. The outcome was that my mum kept on working, which was good for me, as I always got larger portions at lunchtime!

There was even disagreement amongst the women, as the fight for jobs and who should have them came to the fore. Those women who had been widowed by the war, and those who were single, felt that they should be shown a preference over married women.

But as time went on, so many women were in full-time employment that they could no longer be ignored by the unions, and on a practical point of view, the more people a union had in its ranks, men or women, the more money they could collect each month in fees.

In the aftermath of the First World War a strange thing happened, the government brought in the Representation of the People Act 1918. The Act was very well-supported and was passed into law by an overwhelming majority of politicians, with 385 voting for it and only 55 being against it. The Act allowed women who were over the age of 30, and who owned property, the right to vote. There were those who fell into this category from Chelmsford, but it also meant that not all women from the town had the right to vote. The obvious question is why?

As the law stood at the time, only men who had been resident in the country for twelve months prior to an election were eligible to vote. This meant that tens of thousands of servicemen serving overseas might not be allowed to vote. Imagine if you will, how the general election could have turned out if tens of thousands of men had been unable to vote, and every woman over the age of 18, property owner or not, had been able to. The outcome could have been totally different. That's one reason. The strange thing about all of this was the age that women had to be to be eligible to vote. Before the outbreak of the war some suffragettes were of the more militant kind, which I have alluded to elsewhere in the book, they also tended to be slightly older and were generally from the more affluent families of society. Why then give those very same individuals the right to vote? It just doesn't add up as far as I am concerned. Was it because women had in effect kept the country going on the home front throughout the war? Was the Representation of the People Act 1918 the government's way of saying thank you for their efforts during the war? If that was the case, surely they would have given all women who were 18 years of age and older the right to vote, regardless of whether they owned property or not. The issue about a woman owning property and being 30 years of age, certainly wasn't a criteria for women's employment during the war in such occupations as nursing or munitions factories. This then leads to another question, was there a bigger picture in play, that the government simply were not owning up to, that was the real reason for their selectiveness when it came to who was given the right to vote?

In Russia there had been a revolution in 1917 which had seen the collapse of the Russian Empire, the abdication of Emperor

Nicholas, and his subsequent murder along with that of his wife and children. Was the British government worried, scared even, about similar events taking place across Britain? They had seen at first hand just how effective the suffragettes had been at uniting women in a common cause. Most of the leaders and senior figures in the suffragette movement were young middle-class women, who either owned properties or came from affluent families. Maybe, just maybe, it was the government's way of preventing similar events from happening across Britain.

CHAPTER FOUR

First World War

For some people, the name of their loved one on the local war memorial was an all-important factor about how they grieved for their sad loss, taking into account that things were much different, especially in the aftermath of the First World War, when people were, on the whole, expected to just get on with their lives. Many of those who survived their wartime experiences and made it back home to their loved ones, never again spoke of what they had seen and done.

Most war memorials throughout the United Kingdom were not erected until the early years of the 1920s, with additional names being added in the late 1940s for those who had been killed during the Second World War. Most were paid for out of public donations, but had committees to arrange their design, building and erection. These committees ultimately had the final say in relation to the names included on the memorial. In most cases the individuals who sat on these committees were local dignitaries, such as the town's mayor, aldermen, council members, and retired high-ranking military personnel. They would have included very few, if any, of the general public.

There were at least 355 from Chelmsford, mainly men, who were killed or lost their lives as a result of their involvement in the First World War. Most would have been killed in action, whilst some died as a result of their wounds. Others would have died as a result of illness, disease or accidents. Some would have been killed on the home front as a result of German air raids. For each and every one of them there was a mother, possibly a wife, and either female siblings or children, left behind to mourn their passing. There would have been many Chelmsford widows left behind with young children to support, and for most, the only way to achieve this was to remarry.

The reason why I only mention those men who were killed from the First World War and the widows and children that many of them left behind, was because of how life was then. After the First World War, a number of men married war widows, some who had children, which was more remarkable than it might at first appear. Putting aside the war, I wonder how many men would have married a woman, widowed or divorced, and taken on another man's children, in normal times, and if there hadn't been a war on.

VAD Nurses

During the period of the First World War, numerous women from Chelmsford became British Red Cross nurses so that they could do their bit for the war effort. For most, being able to do so while still being able to live in the relative comfort of their own home, and carry on with their normal everyday life, was a very important factor. Many had families to look after, while others had loved ones fighting overseas in the war.

Many of those who volunteered to become nurses were well-educated young women whose middle-class, reasonably affluent families would not suddenly be destitute if one or more of their daughters were not employed in a job where they were bringing home money every week. There were probably a lot more women who wanted to undertake nursing roles for their local VAD section than were in a position to do so, because of social restrictions and family commitments. The fact that so many women were able to become nurses is in itself evidence that a substantial shift had taken place, as far as the progression of women in society was concerned. Women's efforts on the home front during the First World War would lead directly to great advances in women's suffrage. As previously mentioned, the Representation of the People Act 1918 gave the vote to certain women over the age of thirty, because women's wartime contributions could not be ignored by the political establishment.

Prior to the changes, which allowed more men and women to vote, the nation's electorate had been made up of around 8 million rich, well-placed individuals, all of whom would have been property owners. After the Representation of the People Act 1918 the electorate increased to more than 21 million, with 43 per cent of them being women.

The new Act was something tangible. It wasn't a 'hope for the future', 'hot air' or 'empty promises': it was real, it had happened. The lives of women, and the perception of their worth in society, changed so much with the bringing in of that one Act of Parliament. It meant that there could be no going back to what had once been the norm for women. It was a small step on the path to equality, which as it has turned out has been a long road indeed. Prior to the Equality Act 1974 fifty-six years later, women and men were still far from being equal, and a woman would need written permission from her husband to apply for a credit card.

Voluntary Aid Detachments, which were more commonly referred to as VADs, were voluntary units, made up mainly of unpaid workers. Their purpose was to provide nursing services, mainly in hospitals throughout the United Kingdom, although some did serve abroad in different theatres of war.

With political unease and tension on the rise throughout Europe in the early years of the twentieth century, the threat of war became ever more real. With this in mind, in 1909 the Order of St John and the British Red Cross got together to form the Voluntary Aid Detachment system. So much work had been done in the way of organisation and preparation that by the time of the outbreak of the First World War there were some 2,500 separate Voluntary Aid Detachments, with 72,000 volunteers, the vast majority of whom were female. Despite this large pool of readily available volunteers, there were issues and concerns about their actual worth. The military authorities did not want well-meaning individuals working in hospitals near the front line in France and Belgium, but then again, neither did the British Red Cross. They wanted them used and deployed in hospitals on the home front.

There was the added issue of inverted snobbery between the volunteer VAD nurses and the full-time professional nurses, which didn't help the situation either. The sad irony was that the VAD nurses were not trying to take away anybody's job or pretend that they were anything other than what they were: well-meaning volunteers who simply wanted to do their bit. By cleaning wards, changing beds, providing bed baths, bringing the wounded men their meals and hot drinks, they allowed the professional nurses to concentrate on doing what they were best at, which was nursing their patients.

Those who worked for the VAD also cooked or drove ambulances. No matter what role they did, most worked in VAD convalescent hospitals, which was where the wounded soldiers were sent after their wounds had first been treated in a general or a military hospital. Once at the convalescent hospital, all they had to do was to rest and recover from their wounds, so the VAD nurses who were tasked with looking after them didn't have to be medically trained. They offered care and compassion, were good listeners and looked after their patients until they were deemed ready to be discharged and sent back to civvy street, or fit enough to be returned to their units.

By the end of the war a lot of the early discord had been smoothed over, and VAD nurses eventually found themselves working at medical facilities across the Western and Eastern fronts, in Mesopotamia as well as Gallipoli. They provided invaluable service, with many of them being decorated for their work and bravery, while others paid the ultimate price for their volunteer service.

Here is a list of the women from Chelmsford who joined the ranks of the Voluntary Aid Detachments. Most were nurses, but there were also a few who volunteered to help out as cooks, and even a couple as cleaners.

Miss Ida Barton lived in Rainsford Road, Chelmsford. She volunteered to work as a part-time VAD nurse at the outbreak of war in August 1914, and was sent to a Red Cross hospital in

Chelmsford; her service card does not indicate which one. She continued working in Chelmsford until October 1916, when she left to train as a masseuse, and by the end of the war she was working in France as part of the Almeric Paget Massage Corps.

Almeric Paget and his wife, Pauline Payne Whitney, were very well-to-do people, both socially and in a financial sense. At the outbreak of the First World War they approached the War Office in London offering fifty qualified masseuses to work in military hospitals. It was an offer readily accepted. So great was the demand for this type of treatment, that the War Office asked the Pagets to open a day centre in London to help reduce the demand on military hospitals. Due to the generosity of Almeric's parents, Lord and Lady Paget, a clinic was opened in London which could cater for a maximum of 200 men each day. The clinic was located at 55 Portland Place, London, the home of Lord and Lady Paget. So good was the standard of the work carried out by the masseuses of the Almeric Paget Massage Corps that they were also asked to undertake all such similar work in both military hospitals and convalescent camps.

As a result of an inspection in 1916 by the then Director General of the Army Medical Service, Alfred Keogh, the Corps officially had its name changed to the Almeric Paget Military Massage Corps, and its services were paid for by the government. Prior to this the Corps survived on public donations and private funding by the Paget family.

At the beginning of 1917, members of the Corps were allowed to work abroad for the first time, and by the end of the war, fifty-six of the Corps members had volunteered to work overseas. Throughout the war more than 3,300 masseuses and masseurs had worked for the Corps, and at the end of the fighting, 2,000 were still at work. The Almeric Paget Military Massage Corps was finally stood down in January 1919.

Miss Jane Bunn lived at 88 New London Road, Chelmsford. She appears to have been a remarkable character, enlisting as a nurse in the London 214 VAD section in June 1916 when she was 46 years of age. She started work at the St John Auxiliary Hospital in

Fareham, Hampshire, where she remained until September 1916. She then appears to have taken a bit of a break before doing the same role at Chislehurst Auxiliary Military Hospital between 21 February and 21 May 1917. She then took another break before moving on to work at the Military Hospital at Salisbury Plain in Wiltshire, where she began on 2 July 1917 and where she was still working as of 30 May 1919. After examining her VAD service card closely, it would also appear that on 30 May 1921, by which time she was fifty-one years of age, she started working at the Welsh War Hospital at Netley, but when the cards were later typed up, this had been missed off.

Louisa Chennels was 27 years of age and lived at High House, Bloomfield, Chelmsford, when she became a VAD nurse with the Essex 40 section on 21 October 1915. She worked at the 1st Eastern General Hospital, Cambridge, as a part-time nurse. She left there on 21 May 1916 after just seven months, and the British Red Cross holds no other record of her having worked for them after that date. It is of course quite possible that she remained in nursing and simply joined another nursing organisation. Louisa's brother, Morris Chennells, served during the war. He was a private (10134) in the Honourable Artillery Company.

The Meeson family lived at Rettendon Hall Farm in Battlesbridge. William Merryfield Meeson was a farmer and corn merchant, his business making him wealthy enough to employ three servants to look after him, his wife Ellen and their five children. There were four daughters: Edith, Agnes, Mary and Ellen, and a son, Percy. Two of the daughters, Edith and Mary, volunteered to do their bit for the war effort by becoming VAD nurses.

Edith was the eldest of the Meeson children and was 28 at the outbreak of the First World War. She immediately volunteered, joining the Essex VAD 40 section as a full-time unpaid nurse, and was sent to work at the Red Cross Hospital, Chelmsford, where her VAD service card records that 'she had done excellent work'. It also showed that she lived at Rettendon Place and not Rettendon Hall Farm. She was promoted to the position of staff nurse and in May 1915 she was sent to work at Chatham Naval Hospital, where

Above: *NUWSS Badge.*

Right: *VAD Poster.*

Below: *VAD Nurses.*

Almeric Paget Military Massage Corps
COAT AND SKIRT.

The all-round belt is optional.

Skirt to be 6 ins. from ground.

Patch pockets 8 in. long, 8½ in. wide.

Dark blue leather or imitation leather buttons.

Almeric Paget Massage Corps Poster.

Above left: *Mary Kenyon.*

Above right: *Dame Margaret Anstee.*

Below: *Chelmsford High School for Girls, 1913*

CHELMSFORD (HIGHER EDUCATION)
ADVISORY COMMITTEE.

OPENING

OF THE

County High School for Girls,

CHELMSFORD,

ON WEDNESDAY, THE 1st MAY, 1907,

AT 3-30 P.M.,

BY

SIR WM. ANSON, BART., M.P.

GOWERS, LTD., COUNTY PRINTERS, MALDON.

*(Opening ceremony held 5 days before the first pupils
were admitted on Monday 6th May 1907)*

Above: *Chelmsford High
School for Girls, 1907.*

Left: *Opening ceremony of
the school.*

Below: *Headmistress Miss
Edith Bancroft.*

Above left: *Headmistress Miss Geraldine Cadbury.*

Above right: *Woman of the 1850's.*

Right: *Woman of the 1890's.*

Women of 1914.

*Red Cross
Bellefields Hospital,
Chelmsford.*

*Marconi's works,
Chelmsford.*

*Marconi's works,
Chelmsford.*

Above left: *James Billington.*

Above right: *Chelmsford Gaol.*

Right: *Moulsham Street, Chelmsford.*

Right: *A Dames School.*

Below: *Mable Harcourt's wedding certificate*

Above: *A Ragged School.*

Right: *Chelmsford War Memorial.*

Below left: *Working Girls Home, Manchester.*

Below right: *Soldiers Separation Poster.*

she remained until September 1917. It is unclear where she worked after that, possibly back at the Red Cross Hospital, Chelmsford, but she was still serving at the end of the war.

Miss Freda Meeson's VAD service card showed that she also lived at Rettendon Place, but she is not shown on the 1911 census as being one of the four Meeson daughters, and none of the other daughters had a name similar to Freda. I can only assume that either her name has been recorded incorrectly, or she was a niece. She volunteered with the Essex VAD 40 section in August 1914 and went to work at the Red Cross Hospital, Chelmsford as a part-time nurse. She was still serving at the end of the war, by which time she had been awarded her blue efficiency stripe.

Miss Mary Winifred Meeson was 23 years of age at the outbreak of the war, when she volunteered with the Essex VAD 40 section and was initially sent to work at the VAD's Hylands Hospital, Chelmsford, as a part-time nurse, where she remained until January 1915. She appears to have had a few months' break before beginning work at the Red Cross Hospital, Chelmsford, on 11 May 1915. She was still working there at the end of the war, and definitely up to 25 March 1919.

Miss Dorothy Maude Nash lived at 56 Sloane Street, London, although she had previously lived at Broomfields Court in Chelmsford, and served with the London 52 VAD section between 2 May 1917 and January 1919 as a volunteer full-time nurse. During her service she worked at the Ridley House Hospital for Officers at 10 Carlton House Terrace, London SW1, where she worked on the wards. She also worked at the 4th London General Hospital, and at the Lady Gooch Hospital, Chelmsford, which was also referred to as Hylands House Hospital, which was Lord and Lady Gooch's home. She worked full-time for four months between 10 May 1915 and 10 September 1915 at South Devon and East Cornwall General Hospital at Plymouth. She was accepted for military service as a nurse and worked full-time at the 4th London General Hospital, Ruskin Park Extension, Denmark Hill, between November 1915 and June 1916. Her next move took her to the Red Cross Hospital, Chelmsford, possibly the one at New London Road, where she worked full-time for one month from September 1916. From there she moved across town to Hylands House Auxiliary Hospital, where she worked for three months between 1 November 1916 and January 1917, before ending up at the Ridley House Hospital

Miss Catherine Emily Pitts was 36 years of age and living at 203 Springfield Road, Chelmsford, when she became a volunteer full-time nurse working for Essex 40 VAD at the outbreak of the war in August 1914. She was appointed as a senior nurse at the Red Cross Hospital, Chelmsford, where she was credited with having done some excellent work. On 28 June 1917 she was sent to work at the Royal Naval Hospital, Chatham. She was still serving there on 2 October 1919. She died on 5 September 1936 having never married, aged 52, while a patient at Bethlem Hospital, Kent, which was and is a medical facility specialising in psychiatry and mental health issues. In her will she left £7,205 9s 7d. Her younger sister, Miss Edith Mary Pitts, who was 30 years of age and also lived at the family home at 203 Springfield Road, Chelmsford, began working for Essex 40 VAD in August 1914 as a full-time volunteer senior VAD nurse at the Red Cross Hospital, Chelmsford. During her time working there, she carried out some excellent work, having had responsibility for many quite severe cases, while still carrying out her duties efficiently and conscientiously. On 6 October 1917, like her sister Catherine, she went to work at the Royal Naval Hospital, Chatham, where she continued working on a full-time basis. She was still serving there on 2 October 1919, although she did take six weeks off between 13 April and 27 May 1918. Like her sister she died a spinster, on 12 July 1955 in Salterton, Devon. In her will she left £17,034 15s 2d.

Miss Marion Elizabeth Straight was 23 years of age and lived with her widowed mother, Sarah, elder brother, Marshall, her younger sister, Brenda, and servant, Ellen Burrows, at 18 Maltese Road, Woodbury, Chelmsford. In January 1917 she joined the Essex 40 VAD section as a full-time volunteer nurse and was sent to work at the Red Cross Hospital, where she remained until January 1919 when her services were no longer required. Prior to working at the Red Cross Hospital in Chelmsford she had also worked at Writtle House, Writtle.

Miss Brenda Straight, who was the younger sister of Marion (above), was 18 years of age when she began working as a full-time volunteer nurse for Essex 40 VAD in March 1916 at the Red Cross Hospital in Chelmsford. This was a position she remained in until the early months of January 1919 when her services were no longer required. Marshall Stuart Straight, brother to Marion and Brenda, served in the army during the First World War. Initially with the 11th Canadian Infantry as a sergeant (21885), he then received a commission and became a second lieutenant with the 12th Battalion, Essex Regiment. He was later attached to the 1st Battalion. Along with his colleagues, Marshall landed at Cape Helles, Gallipoli, on 25 April 1915. He was killed in action on 24 December 1915 and is buried at Lancashire Landing Cemetery in Turkey. I wonder if Marion and Brenda's decision to serve with the VAD was influenced by the loss of their brother.

As can be seen from some of the entries above, the VAD section that most of the women worked for was the same. There were numerous sections, or units, scattered throughout Essex, some of which had been in place since 1909. There were both male and female VAD units. The male units were allocated odd numbers, and the women even. Chelmsford men were allocated the reference Essex VAD 3, while the women were allocated numbers 4 and 40. Essex VAD 4 was Chelmsford A, and Essex VAD 40 was Chelmsford B.

How did women cope with their husbands going off to war? Those families who had children usually had more than one child. So a wife would have been without her husband and her only contact with him would have been via the pages of a letter. Sadly, for many husbands and wives, when the time came to say goodbye they would be destined never to see each other again. In many cases the final resting place of their husband would be in a cemetery in a town, the name of which they had possibly never heard of before. They were buried in a far off place, in another country, where wives and families could never afford to go and visit. For most, all they had to remember their husband by was his name commemorated on the local war memorial.

The issue was, how did wives manage financially when their husbands went to war? Some went out and got themselves a job, either part-time or full-time, but wives and children of married men who had gone off to fight in the war were also entitled to Soldiers' Separation Allowances, the rates of which were increased from 1 March 1915. The same was also available to the dependants of unmarried men. The amount of money a soldier's wife was paid depended on two things; how many children she had and what rank her husband was. By way of example, if a wife had no children and her husband was of the rank of private or corporal, she would receive 12s 6d per week. If she had one child that would rise to 17s 6d, and if she had two children it would be 21s. For each additional child, she would receive 2s. At the other end of the scale, the wife of a Warrant Officer 1st Class, would receive 23s per week. If she had a child that amount would rise to 28s, and if she had two children, she would receive 31s 6d.

These allowances also included adopted children, some of which could have quite conceivably have been the children of a soldier who had been killed. The upper age limit for children was 16-years-old, although in certain cases, such as the child being in higher education, serving an apprenticeship on a nominal wage, or suffering from a physically or mental infirmity, payments could continue until they were 21 years of age.

All of the above was dependent on the soldier having been married prior to him having enlisted. If a soldier married after he had enlisted, then none of the entitlements were available to his wife and any children that they subsequently had. An additional payment of 3s 6d was paid in the case of a soldier living in the London postal area at the time of his enlistment, as long as his family continued to live there. If a soldier's wife had died, there was then a payment of 5s a week for each child.

If a soldier who was either unmarried, a widower, or whose wife was not drawing separation allowance because they had been living apart from before the war, had anyone, related or not, actually dependent on him from before he enlisted, the government would pay that dependant a weekly sum of money, providing that the soldier contributed a share to the amount paid. This included children.

The Chelmsford Civic War Memorial commemorates the names of 391 men who were from or who had connections to the town, and who died as a result of their involvement in the First World War. There are other war memorials at Broomfield, Springfield, Moulsham, and Widford, although many of the men who are commemorated on these memorials, are also recorded on the Chelmsford one.

There were hundreds more who had enlisted in the armed forces, who survived and made it home, this means that there were potentially hundreds of wives and children of soldiers, living in Chelmsford during the war who were reliant on Soldiers' Separation Allowances, to survive the four long, bloody and harsh years of the First World War.

If a married woman lost her husband as a result of their involvement in the war, they were covered by the War Pensions Act 1914. This didn't mean, by any stretch of the imagination, that widows would then be paid a pension for the rest of their days. Most of these pensions lasted for a set period of time, some no longer than a year.

The number of servicemen from Great Britain who died or were reported as being missing in action during the First World War, has been estimated at 750,000. Of these, some 240,000 were married, which meant that there were the same number of widows, and, if we say each family had two children, that would mean that nearly half a million children were growing up without a father. Going back to the 391 men who are commemorated on the Chelmsford war memorial who were lost to the war. If we use the national average of a third of those being married, that would mean that Chelmsford had approximately 130 war widows, and 260 children who had lost their father.

In Jonathan Swan's book, *Chelmsford in the Great War*, he makes mention of some 1,791 men who had served in either the army or navy throughout the course of the war.

Being a widow with a number of children was a difficult situation to be in. Most would have been from the working classes, who would have been dependent on their husbands wage to pay for food, clothes and the rent for the property that they lived in. If fortunate enough to find another suitor, who was prepared to take her and her children on, with an offer of marriage, very few women would be in a position to turn it down, even if they didn't actually love the man they were to marry. The alternative option wasn't a pleasant one to contemplate, as it usually involved the workhouse.

Social convention of the day determined that following the death of a husband, there should be a period of time for mourning. A widow failing to adhere to this custom risked being seen as an unfaithful widow in the eyes of her neighbours and the wider community.

Losing a husband to the war had a devastating effect on a grieving wife and her family. The impact wasn't just an emotional one, but also a financial one. Average pay for a man was 26 shillings per week, whereas a women doing the same job, for the same amount of hours, was only paid 11 shillings per week, therefore a wife losing her husband's wage inevitably caused great hardship to the family.

If a woman married an ex-soldier after he had been discharged from the army, and he subsequently died of his wounds or illness which he had sustained whilst serving in the war, she was not entitled to a widow's pension.

Even when a widow had been awarded a pension, she wasn't totally safe, as they could be revoked by the Local Pensions Office. Grounds for doing this varied; drunkenness was most certainly frowned upon, as was neglecting their children. Living with another man out of wedlock definitely brought with it a social stigma, and was not the kind of reputation most women would want to acquire.

Mrs Annie Rolfe from Chelmsford had six of her sons serving in the Armed Forces during the course of the First World War, having already lost her husband in an accident at work in November 1901. Annie had borne her husband nine children in total. George Rolfe died in a tragic accident at the town gasworks, where he worked as a stoker, on Friday, 1 November 1901. He was just 44 years of age, and his death left his widow to bring up their children on her own.

At the inquest into George's death, the jury, having heard all the relevant evidence, determined that his death had taken place due to 'accidental suffocation brought about by fumes rising from the valve chamber at the works'.

In 1909 Annie married again, to a man named Alfred Philpott, but when war broke out in 1914 six of her sons enlisted to serve their country.

The 1901 census listed the following members of the Rolfe family:

George Rolfe,	41 years of age
Annie Rolfe,	40 years of age
Arthur Rolfe,	17 years of age
William Rolfe,	15 years of age
Fred Rolfe,	13 years of age
Johnnie Rolfe,	10 years of age
Florrie Rolfe,	8 years of age
Frank Rolfe,	6 years of age
Charles Rolfe,	3 years of age
Reuben Rolfe,	1 year of age

The family were shown as living at 2 Provident Square, Springfield, Chelmsford. Annie Louisa Rolfe, the ninth child of the family, wasn't born until 20 August 1901, just nine weeks before the death of her father.

Frank Rolfe was a corporal (209317) in the Royal Air Force. He survived the war but died on 12 December 1918, as a result of pneumonia after having fallen ill as part of the worldwide flu pandemic.

William enlisted in the Army on 22 May 1915 at Chelmsford and became a private (35107) in the 3rd Battalion, Essex Regiment. He was 33 years of age at the time, although he had previously served in the Royal Garrison Artillery in the years before the outbreak of war. He became an acting lance corporal on 4 April 1916 before being fully promoted to the rank on 4 November 1916.

He was posted to the regiment's 13th Battalion on 5 January 1917 before being promoted to the rank of sergeant four months later on 29 April. The final year of the war would prove to be a strange affair for William. He was posted to B Company, 9th Battalion on 10 February 1918, before being officially reported as 'missing in the field' on 27 March, although his next of kin were not informed until 25 April. However, on 31 March the Germans confirmed to the British authorities that William had in fact been captured and was a prisoner of war. At the end of hostilities he was released and returned to England, arriving home on 21 November 1918. He was demobbed on 18 February 1919, at which time he was shown as living at 111 Mildmay Road, Chelmsford, with his wife, Annie Bertha Rolfe, whom he had married at Chelmsford Register Office on 27 February 1911, and their four children, Winifred, Dorothy, William and Beatrice, the latter being born on 4 August 1914.

It would have been an extremely difficult time for all of his family and friends during the period of time that he was reported missing in action, and before it had been confirmed by the Germans that he had been captured and was, in fact, a prisoner of war. It would have been a traumatic time for his mother, who already had to deal with the constant worry of having six sons serving. It must have been a similar experience for his wife, who was not only worried about what had happened to her husband, but if William had been killed, what this would have ultimately meant for their four young children. His wife Annie was so concerned for his wellbeing that on 10 April 1918 she wrote a letter to the Essex Regiment, part of which said, 'I should deem it a great favour if you could let me have any news of my husband, as I have not heard from him for a month. I keep writing every day, but I have received no answer.'

William's case was replicated not only elsewhere in Chelmsford, but across the length and breadth of the country, with mothers and wives beside themselves with grief, waiting to hear if their husbands and sons were safe and well. Although not exact figures, the Commonwealth War Graves Commission website records that more than 600 people, mostly men, from Chelmsford lost their lives during the course of the First World War, and more than 200 men and women from the town lost their lives during the years of the Second World War. Add to this those men who were wounded, or captured and taken as prisoners of war, and that resulted in an awful lot of worry for the women of Chelmsford.

A quick glance at the Civil Registration Marriage Index for England and Wales for the period 1916–2005, shows that Chelmsford weddings from 1916 through 1920 make for interesting reading:

1916 – 563
1917 – 587
1918 – 662
1919 – 726
1920 – 772

A percentage of the Chelmsford women included in these figures would have been war widows, possibly with the future of their children to consider, in a situation which did not affect men in the same way. It's interesting to note that in 1919 and 1920 there was an increase in the number of couples who were married in the Chelmsford area, immediately after the end of the war.

CHAPTER FIVE

Second World War

In some respects the Second World War mirrored the First in relation to what women contributed to the war effort on the home front. They still had to deal with the worry of their loved ones away fighting in the war, whether that was a husband, father or son. They had to go about their everyday lives as best they could, but just twenty years after the end of the First World War, the world had become so much more developed. Horses were no longer an integral part of military life, and the Second World War certainly wouldn't see the British Army undertaking any cavalry charges. Aviation had dramatically improved. There were no more zeppelins or flimsily made bi-planes, these had long ago been replaced by large bomber aircraft that could carry massive payloads, with some of their bombs weighing 500 pounds. There were also fast-moving fighter planes with automatic machine guns that spewed out hot, molten lead at a frightening rate, from both of their wings.

As in the previous war, women in the Second World War once again played a vital role, only this time some had no choice in the matter.

In May 1939, as part of the Military Training Act, the government had announced plans for limited conscription for single men aged between 20 and 22 years of age. On 3 September 1939, this was amended by the implementation of The National Service (Armed Forces) Act 1939, which imposed conscription on all males, married or single, who were between the ages of 18 and 41. Those men working who were employed in the baking industry, farming, engineering and the medical profession, were exempt as these men were deemed to be working in 'key industries.'

As this is a book about women, you might be wondering why I am writing about conscription in the Second World War. Well, a little-known fact was that women also faced conscription as a result of a second National Service Act in December 1941. The women it affected were those aged between 20 and 30, and this included all unmarried women and childless widows. The reason why women now faced conscription was that there were insufficient numbers of women volunteering for auxiliary units of the armed forces.

Women were given the option of working in industry, such as munitions factories, or joining one of the country's auxiliary services, of which there were three: The Auxiliary Territorial Service (ATS); the Women's Auxiliary Air Force (WAAF); or the Women's Royal Naval Service (WRNS). Those who chose the ATS initially undertook such roles as cooks, clerks, orderlies, working in stores, dispatch riders or drivers, but as the war continued their work could also include serving in anti-aircraft batteries. Some 250,000 women served in the ATS during the Second World War.

Women serving in the WAAF carried out a variation of roles including compiling important weather reports, the maintaining of aircraft and intelligence work. The number of women who served with them was 182,000.

There were some 75,000 women working for the WRNS, some of whom served overseas, whilst some worked at Bletchley Park where the code-breaking work took place.

Although women's conscription was introduced due to the lack of women volunteers for these branches of the military, the flip side was that the type of work they did allowed men who had previously been undertaking these roles to be released for front line duties. Maybe that was the plan all along.

There were other roles that women could do, but these were voluntary and weren't covered by conscription. These included working for the First Aid Nursing Yeomanry (FANY), so called because when they were initially founded in 1907, they were on horseback and were a link between soldiers wounded on the front line and the field hospitals. They were the equivalent of a combat medic of today. The Women's Voluntary Service (WVS) were involved with the evacuation of civilians from urban areas. They handed out food, drink, and warm clothing to troops returning from Dunkirk.

During the Blitz they set up mobile canteens which provided food and drink to the overworked firemen and ARP wardens, fighting the numerous fires, quite often in extremely dangerous situations. They also ran incident inquiry points, which were locations where members of the public came to find out about their loved ones who were missing as a result of the bombings. They assisted with the sometimes emotive subject of food rationing; in the build-up to D-Day their efforts to help feed the tens of thousands of Allied soldiers waiting to make their way across the English Channel, was invaluable. Some also worked overseas during the war as well. By 1941 alone, an estimated 1 million women had already served with the WVS in some capacity.

Some women opted to volunteer for the Civil Defence, others for the National Fire Service, or the Air Transport Auxiliary, the latter of which was a particularly exciting role. It involved flying new, repaired and damaged military aircraft, between factories, maintenance units, active service squadrons, and assembly plants. They were also used, in urgent cases, as an air ambulance, and to ferry senior military personnel who were engaged on important and urgent matters.

A number of women from Chelmsford and the surrounding districts were involved working with some of these units. The possible reason for the lack of expected numbers enlisting into either the military units or the voluntary organisations was that between 1936 and 1940, there was a year-on-year rise in the numbers of women from the Chelmsford area who were married. The following four years, up to and including 1944, saw a decline in the number of marriages, possibly because of the uncertainty which came with the war. Between 1945 and 1948 the average number of women who were married in Chelmsford was 1,271.

In the early years of the war in particular, families would spend entire evenings sleeping in air-raid shelters because of the real and present danger of night time air-raids by German bombers. Such attacks became a reality in Chelmsford because of what were classed as legitimate military targets, in the form of the factories at Marconi Wireless and Hoffmann's ball bearings. These were targeted raids by the Luftwaffe, not random attacks by enemy aircraft who wanted to jettison their remaining munitions before starting their journey back home to Germany.

These air raids resulted in the deaths of men, women and children who lived in Chelmsford. According to the lists kept of civilian deaths during the years of the Second World War, a total of 161 ordinary people from Chelmsford died during that time, although not all of them were as a result of enemy air raids.

The list of women below has little to do with women's suffrage in its truest sense, but these were all ordinary women who paid the ultimate price. Some were killed in the work place, while others were in what should have been the comfort and security of their own homes. Every one of them knew the risks they were taking by staying in Chelmsford, especially those who lived near to, or were working for the Hoffmann Ball Bearing Factory or the Marconi Wireless Telegraph Company, both of which were legitimate military targets for the Germans to attack.

In the days before laser-guided missiles, rockets and bombs could not be dispatched to their intended targets with pinpoint accuracy. Dropping bombs was only as effective as the skills of those tasked with despatching them. If they got it wrong, by just a matter of yards, the consequences would often be catastrophic.

These women were civilians; normal people going about their everyday business during a time of war. Some of them were engaged in wartime military related work at the time of their deaths. They weren't working at military instillations or in munitions factories in support of the war effort, but a number of them were working at the Hoffmann Ball Bearing Factory and the Marconi Wireless Telegraph Company, both of which carried out work for military purposes during both World Wars.

Other businesses who employed women in the town, particularly during the war years, were Crompton Electrical Engineering, which was located at a factory known as the 'Arc Works' in Writtle Road, Chelmsford. It had been there since 1895, although it was first established at Queen Street in the town in 1878. Crompton's were pioneers of electric street lighting and electric traction engines. Also the English Electric Valve Company, which began life as part of the Marconi Group in the early years of the Second World War, and as it was involved in the manufacture of magnetrons for defence radar systems, it was most definitely a target of the German Luftwaffe.

Alice Maud Emery was 41 years of age when she was killed during an air raid on Sunday, 13 October 1940. She worked for the town's mayor, John Thompson, as a live-in servant at his home, Brierley Place, New London Road, Chelmsford. The house suffered a direct hit from one of the bombs dropped by the Luftwaffe. The mayor, his wife, Emma Thompson, their son, Lieutenant-Colonel Thomas Thompson, and the mayor's grandchildren, Audrey Mary Thompson, who was 8 years of age, and Diana Louisa Thompson, who was just 14-months-old, all died in the same attack. Alice, along with all the members of the Thompson family, was buried at the Chelmsford Municipal Borough Cemetery.

Winifred Gowen was 39 years of age and lived at 26 Coval Lane, Chelmsford, which was part of a block of flats, with her husband Arnold and her 9-year-old son, Barry. She and Barry were killed in the early hours of 21 May 1941, along with five others, when a bomb landed on the block of flats at Coval Lane. Fortunately for Arnold, he was working a night shift at the Hoffmann Works on the night in question. The Commonwealth War Graves Commission states that Winifred and her son were both buried at Chelmsford Municipal Borough Cemetery. But an article on page 4 of the *Chelmsford Chronicle* dated Friday, 30 May 1941 describes the joint funeral of Winifred and Barry Gowen having taken place on Tuesday, 27 May 1941 at Braintree Cemetery. The Reverend Hartley Brook, the Vicar of Braintree, officiated at the funeral service. The following 'Memoriam' appeared on the front page of the *Chelmsford Chronicle* dated Friday, 15 May 1942, placed by Arnold.

In loving memory of my dear wife, Winifred Gowen aged 39 years, also my dear son, Barry John Gowen, aged 9 years, who were killed by enemy action on May 20th-21st, 1941. 'Great the shock, and severe. To part with those I loved so dear: Only those who have lost can tell. The suffering in parting without farewell.' Always in my thoughts, but safe in God's keeping.

Mrs Louisa Mary Rolfe was 61 years of age and living at 29 Roman Road, Chelmsford, when she died at Chelmsford Hospital of injuries received in an explosion on the evening of Wednesday, 6 May 1942. She had been visiting her daughter, Mrs Winifred Harrhy, who lived at 35 Navigation Road, Chelmsford. She was buried at the Chelmsford Municipal Borough Cemetery. Mrs Rolfe's death was not the last of the family's tragedies, as her husband, Frederick John Rolfe, who was 66 years of age, died just thirteen days later on Tuesday, 19 May 1942. According to the *Essex Newsman* newspaper dated Saturday, 23 May 1942, Frederick died 'very suddenly' and 'passed peacefully to his rest' at Chelmsford Hospital on Tuesday, 19 May 1942. Despite his wife having been buried at the town's Municipal Borough Cemetery, the newspaper report said that Frederick was buried at Writtle Road Cemetery, Chelmsford, on Saturday, 23 May 1942, after a funeral service at St John's Church in Chelmsford. The *Chelmsford Chronicle*, dated Friday, 29 May 1942, provided a slightly different account of Mr Rolfe's death. According to their report of his inquest, he met his death after a fall at Hoffmann's Works, where he was employed. Mr and Mrs Rolfe's son, John Rolfe, said that his mother's death had come as a great shock to his father, who was then off work for some twelve days, as he gradually came to terms with his loss. He only returned to work on 18 May and he was described by some of his colleagues as being 'quiet' and 'depressed', both of which would be reasonable descriptions of somebody who had suffered the tragic and unexpected loss of a loved one. The coroner, Mr Beccle, returned a verdict of accidental death.

Mrs Ellen May Wrenn, who was 28 years of age and lived at 43 Henry Road, Chelmsford, was killed by enemy action on the morning of Monday, 19 October 1942, when a bomb intended for the nearby Hoffmann Works, exploded outside her home. The Commonwealth War Graves website shows that besides Mrs Wrenn, the following people died that day as a result of the air raid: Mr Andrew Fenwick, aged 25, who lived at 45 Henry Road, Chelmsford; Elizabeth Locke, who was 57 years of age and who lived at 44 Henry Road; David Alan Westrip, who was 10 years of age, killed at 17 Henry Road; and Albert Radley, aged 35, and Denis Wyatt, aged 28, both killed while working at the nearby Hoffman Works.

My apologies if I have missed anyone out, but if I have then it isn't through lack of research. Although all the deaths have their own tragic story, the nineteen women who died whilst working at the Hoffmann Ball Bearing Factory, in the early hours of Tuesday, 19 December 1944, highlight the progression made regarding the employment of women over the course of time; if not for the war then these would have been roles still undertaken by men. These nineteen women died proving that they were just as capable as their male counterparts of doing the same job, as they had done during the years of the First World War.

In the summer of 1940, an emergency hospital was set up at New Hall, Boreham, Chelmsford, which could cater for 270 patients, most of whom were elderly and had been transferred there from the Suttons Institution at Hornchurch. The need to move all of the patients had come about as a result of the Air Ministry requisitioning the Suttons Institution for military purposes. Many of the hospital's staff had also made the move although some local Chelmsford women began working there as well.

On Saturday, 1 May 1943, the wedding of Miss Kathleen Birch, of 88 West Avenue, Chelmsford, and Sapper Leonard Cottis of the Royal Engineers, who was also from Chelmsford, took place at Chelmsford Cathedral. Leonard's father gave his new daughter-in-law away in the unavoidable absence of her own father, Staff Sergeant J. O'Shea, who was serving overseas and who was, sadly for him and his daughter, not in a position to return to the UK in time for the wedding.

The bride wore a small check-design dress, with fox fur trimmings, and she carried a spray of pink carnations and an ivory coloured prayer book. Miss Joan Cottis, sister of the bridegroom, was the bridesmaid, and was also carrying a spray of pink carnations. On leaving the church, the bride and the newly anointed Mrs Cottis were presented with a silver horseshoe by her colleagues from a local factory.

It was reassuring that despite the times people were living in, marriages still took place, couples hadn't been totally put off by the war and the horrors that came with it. Nobody knew what the future held, how long the war would continue for, and which side was going to win. In Kathleen's case it was even more relevant, as with Leonard being in the army, she didn't know how much time they had together before he would leave for the front. These were difficult times for everybody, but love was an unbreakable bond for some and the desire to live for the day, not knowing if it was going to be their last together, was even stronger.

Chelmsford suffered both death and destruction as a result of numerous German air raids which intentionally targeted the town throughout the course of the Second World War. The worst of the raids took place on Friday, 14 May 1943 when the hospital was attacked by German aircraft. What the pilots thought they were bombing isn't known, but two high explosive bombs were dropped, both scoring direct hits on the hospital buildings. Seven people were killed outright with a further four subsequently dying of their wounds.

The scars and memories of the First World War were still fresh in the minds of many people who had lost close family members, some who had lost their own fathers when they themselves had been young children. The 'war to end all wars' was the phrase of the time, but here they were just twenty years later with history repeating itself. Many wives had become widows and struggled to bring up their children, some did it on their own, whilst others remarried to provide those children with the security that they deserved. Now the children had become adults and it was the turn of the daughters to be mothers and wives. For many, it was the experience of what they had seen their own mothers go through that made them stronger to endure the same, a memory that they could now call upon in their own hour of need.

Chelmsford also had St John's Hospital, situated at Wood Street on the opposite side of town, which had originally opened in 1837 as an infirmary to the local workhouse, and finally closed completely on 18 November 2010.

A lady by the name of Mary Kenyon went on to work at Bletchley Park during the Second World War. She was assigned to the Registration Room, collecting, collating and organising signals. I have included a comprehensive and much more detailed piece about her, which is included in the chapter on Chelmsford's famous women.

There are 177 names of men from Chelmsford, recorded and commemorated on the town's war memorial, who were killed and died whilst serving in the military during the course of the Second World War. It has been said that the average age of a combat soldier during those years was 26. With that in mind, a number of the men recorded on the town's war memorial would have been married, which once again meant that a number of women from Chelmsford were widowed by war.

During the Second World War, fallen British military personnel overseas were rarely brought home to be buried. Travel was difficult and few people could arrange to visit the last resting place of their loved one. In September 1948 Mrs Pamela Margaret Gwendoline Stoney, who lived at Friars Flats, Moulsham Street, Chelmsford decided to make a pilgrimage to Arnhem in Holland to see the grave of her husband, Driver T/14264139 Denis Breading, who was only 21 years of age when he was killed in action on Tuesday, 19 September 1944. He is buried at the Arnhem Oosterbeek War Cemetery in Holland.

The trip was an annual event organised by the Airborne Forces Security Fund. Relatives paid just £10 towards the total cost of the travel and accommodation. Everything else was paid for by the fund.

Mrs Stoney had only been married to Private Breading for seven months when he was killed at Arnhem while serving with the

Royal Army Service Corps, attached to the 253rd Company, First Airborne Division. While in Holland, Mrs Stoney stayed with the Dutch family of a little boy who tended her husband's grave. Each grave was cared for by a Dutch boy who lived in the Arnhem or Oosterbeek area.

The trip took place between 14 and 19 September 1948, which meant that for Mrs Stoney it was exactly four years after the death of her husband. The friends and loved ones of those who were killed were accompanied on the trip by servicemen who had taken part in the landings and survived.

Below are the wedding figures for women from Chelmsford, covering the period from 1936 to 1948. What is really noticeable is that the figures don't change that much at all, which includes, before, during and after the war:

1936 – 943
1937 – 995
1938 – 1,098
1939 – 1,429
1940 – 1,470
1941 – 1,325
1942 – 1,261
1943 – 1,036
1944 – 963
1945 – 1,316
1946 – 1,241
1947 – 1,206
1948 – 1,320

It would appear that the attitude of both men and women hadn't changed that much throughout the war when, understandably, couples didn't know if they would ever see each other again once the man had enlisted and gone off to war. So, the attitude tended to be, live for the moment and live it to the full, rather than wait for a clearer and more secure future, which may never have been. Once the war was over, the number of marriages continued in the same vein, as couples looked forward to a brighter future and a better tomorrow after having survived nearly six years of war, some of which saw them separated.

When writing such books, now and again I come across a real gem of a story, a story that encompasses everything that I want to say. The following is one such story. It belongs to a lady by the name Olive Cox, and is her account of her wartime memories. My thanks to Olive's granddaughter Marie-Ann Capps for giving me her permission to include this intimate account. Olive's account of her wartime memories was written on 2 July 1995, when she was 81 years of age. She passed away in 2009, aged 95.

I was a nursemaid at a house in Stock, Essex when the war started. I had a boyfriend called Dennis since I was 16-years-old. In 1942, the house being large, it was made into a girls school and I came back to Chelmsford, Essex to live.

My friend was going into the ATS (Auxiliary Territorial Army – Women) and I wanted to go with her. My father said no. If I wanted to do war work I could go to Hoffmann's, makers of Ball Bearings or Marconi's both in Chelmsford, Essex. So I chose Hoffmann's as my Dad was already working there.

The hours were 7.30 am – 5.15 pm with 1 hour for dinner, 7.30 am – 11 am on Saturday mornings. We had to work at least two nights a week overtime until 7.30pm with half an hour break. Looking back the days seemed long. The glass roof was blacked out for obvious reasons, so we saw very little daylight.

Steel came into the Turret view (where my father worked) and was cut to various sizes and round shapes, then into the Grinding shop and view where my sister worked. All the rough edges were ground down and polished and then passed on to the Batching view where the bearings were laid in trays all the same size. Lastly they were sent to Final view where I worked and measured the accuracy of the finished bearings. There is an outer and an inner case, I measured the latter. Then onto Lapping view where the two were assembled plus the balls etc.

Over the age of 18 years I had to work nights. Six nights of 12 hours with 1 hour for dinner, 11-12 midnight. In the fields near the factory was a Barrage Balloon site plus airmen. We used to spend our dinner break in their hut drinking tea, etc, often watching the Balloon go up and down if there was an Air Raid. The money was good. I went from 18 shillings and 6 pence (about 85p) to £7 plus bonuses of £1.50. It was a lot of money to us. My stepmother complained that I earned more than my father.

We had ration books.

2 oz tea

4 oz sugar. When available (I have drunk tea without sugar from that day.)

2 oz butter

4 oz meat

1 egg per week

1 box powdered egg

I never handled Ration Books. We never learnt to cook, partly as there was no time, and food could not be wasted.

There was a lot of bombing in Chelmsford. Mostly planes dropping bombs in surrounding fields if they could not reach London. There were Barrage Balloons right up to the outskirts of London. Hoffmann's did have a couple of bomb attacks and damage and casualties, but I was never in the building at the time.

We had a big Anderson shelter in the house about 10 ft square, steel topped with mesh sides and we used to sleep in that if the sirens went. It had to serve as a table because it took up all the space.

We often had evacuees down from the East End. Mothers and small children. They complained about being in the country, hated the fields and scuttled back to London as soon as possible. We also had service men billeted in our houses, Polish Airmen, soldiers etc. They came to Marconi's on courses. Radar was just being invented. They would stay for about a month and wives would come to see them if they were married. As they were Armed Forces, they received extra rations.

I became engaged to Dennis in 1942 and he was called up for the Army and sent to Africa. Across in Sicily he was injured in a lorry accident and was sent home in 1944. End of the Army. When he recovered he was a carpenter and was sent to East London to repair the houses. At this time we had another boarder who worked at Marconi's on secret things. He wasn't allowed to talk about anything. I think a German Battleship had been sunk by this new Radar Equipment.

My sister Rene was younger than me. At this time American soldiers and Airmen had begun to arrive at airfields etc. around Chelmsford, Boreham, Dunmow and Wethersfield. Their allowances were much higher than our soldiers and the town soon filled up on Friday and Saturday nights. Little khaki jeeps were everywhere. They seemed to have an unlimited supply of petrol or gas. My sister met one called John and had a great time. Lorries would come into town and take the girls out to their camps for dancing and food. Eventually she was allowed to bring John home. He came laden with butter, cheese, coffee (we had never drunk so much coffee), bacon and sweets for us. Needless to say he was very welcome.

Rene and John used to go to dinner at the Strand Palace Hotel in London and dancing at Rainbow Corner in Piccadilly. As I was engaged to Dennis I would not take part in these outings. John's brother Andy was a Flying Officer lately arrived and wanted to take me out. (Looking back Andy is now a millionaire with his own very successful business with his and hers Cadillacs in the garage.)

This was now 1944 with D-Day around the corner. John was sent over to France. He and others fashioned runways and hangars in airfields, laying miles of concrete, having already built the Boreham and Dunmow airfields. Andy was sent to Peterborough and we came back to ordinary rations and no sweets. Life was hard.

Bulletins came over the factory radio and also we had Workers' Playtime *every day. I worked amongst about 100 girls and everyone sang to the latest songs with Vera Lynn and Ann Shelton and hosts of other stars. By the way, we still had our hush-hush lodger whose name was Leslie. My stepmother had friends in Bournemouth and in September 1944 went down to stay for a holiday. This was the time of "Doodle Bugs", aircraft with no pilots which crash landed on London and Southern England day and night. Although we felt we were winning the war, these were unknown nightmares doing a lot of damage. The war of the Atlantic when so many merchant ships were sunk, seemed to have finished. A great deal of German submarines were sunk. Also, the ports in Germany where they were made, were heavily bombed. Wilhemshaven and along the Kiel Canal were prime targets. Also the infamous V2 rockets were coming over which were here before the sirens went and could not be detected. These added a new dimension to the war.*

My stepmother wrote to say she was coming home and could we meet her at Waterloo Station. Leslie said he would be pleased to escort me and I managed to get off work and we caught a train to London and thence to Waterloo to await my Stepmother's arrival at 8.45 pm. Unknown to us, she had caught an earlier train and got herself home.

The air raid sirens and explosions and gunfire banged around us, most rail stations were closed so we had to stay on Waterloo Station all night with no food or drink. We arrived back home the next morning very tired, etc. I also had to account for my time off.

Christmas 1944 came and went and Leslie and myself became in those days 'better acquainted.' He was ten years older than myself and my father suggested I found 'someone of my own age'. By now I had broken my engagement with Dennis for this new love of my life. My stepmother asked Leslie to find somewhere else to live and when I said I would go too, she said no more about it. By this time I was on night work six nights a week, which did not leave much time for a social life. When I got home in the morning, Leslie had already left for work.

On 21 December 1944 a two ton rocket dropped on the war factory killing about forty people. My father was then on night work and I went down with Leslie to try and find him. Most of the houses around were down or damaged. Christmas decorations all over the roads. Lots of people trying to stop sightseers but knowing the layout of the different floors in the factory I left Leslie and eventually found my Dad shocked but unhurt. The nurses around said I could walk him slowly home which was about a mile away and we eventually arrived there. He insisted on going to work the next night, but he seemed to have changed overnight.

Eventually winter turned to spring. Allied troops were fighting along all fronts towards Germany with the Russians fighting from the East. It became a time of joy with every day some new victory announced. We had radio bulletins every hour and lots of cheering through the departments. The last months of the war I had been transferred to the

Small Arms department, testing and inspecting rifle bullets. This was in complete darkness with lights only over the cubicles in which we worked. March and April were warm months. I still remember my five minute breaks to stand out in the sun.

By this time the rocket sites had been found and heavily bombed at Peenemünde so they had almost ceased. All the airfields around were very busy. All day and night, Flying Fortresses in large formations flew over the town with Marauder fighters as escorts with the large white star on. When they returned red flares were thrown out if there were dead or injured on board. One thousand bomber raiders we watched go out at dusk when there was no moon. Wonderful sights.

Every day we had bulletins with our Workers' Playtime. *During late April the rockets had all ceased. The big event locally was the wedding of the girl next door. Coupons were scrounged for material for the dress. We used to go to the market on Saturdays and tell the stall holders we worked at Hoffmann's and we could buy clothes without coupons. We had twenty to last six months and a coat was eighteen, so we cultivated our own Black Market very successfully. Anyway, the wedding was a huge success. We kept chickens so six eggs went for the cake. The neighbours gave small amounts of butter and sugar. We sure wished John was around with the PX rations. Anyway, a large cake was produced and we all tasted it and it was good.*

End of April the weather was hot. I was then on night work so I saw some of the lovely weather. All getting excited as the war seemed to be ending. Italy had been invaded and almost defeated. Most of the Army had surrendered. I think the Dictator, Mussolini, had been captured and hung upside down from a pole. We were joyful.

I have not mentioned the Far East War. We heard only what Churchill and the government considered was good for morale. He gave a very sad radio broadcast on the fall of Singapore in 1942. We heard of two large battleships sunk in the China Seas, with great loss of life. The 14th Army was sent to Burma to block the Japanese advance to India. Prisoners were taken in vast amounts and we only learnt the full horror of their imprisonment after the war. I personally knew one soldier, 6 ft 2 in tall who came home weighing 6 stone. He said there were thousands like him. At least he managed to stay alive

to come home, as men died of starvation, dysentery, etc. all around
him. This was mostly the Americans war with all the Pacific Islands
being fought over most savagely.

The Japanese thought it an honour to die for their country with
of course huge casualties on both sides. But during April the Allied
powers seemed to be getting the upper hand. The Jap Armies never
reached India or Australia, I praise be.

Beginning of May, the River Rhine had been crossed from the West
and the Russians were heading to Berlin from the East. Our papers
were about five pages thick but we read every word. Church Bells
sounded for different victories. They had been silenced for the duration
to ring only for an invasion. First week in May flew past.

May 7th – Fall of Berlin. Crazy, crazy time.

May 8th – Germany surrendered.

I did not go to work that day and neither did Leslie. We caught a
train to London and walked from Liverpool Street station right along
past St Paul's and bomb damaged City to the Strand, which was full of
people singing and dancing down the Strand toward Trafalgar Square.
I think what buses there were gave up the struggle.

The Square was just a mass of people with soldiers etc. sleeping
in doorways and curb sides with their rifles propping up their kit
bags. Everyone has seen the newsreels lately. Well I was there! We
danced, we sang and joined hands in a huge crocodile down to
Whitehall and Mr Churchill and the Government came out on the
Treasury balcony to a huge roar of voices. He gave his Victory sign
and we blew him kisses and laughed and shouted. London had never
seen the like.

The crocodiles of solid masses of people then wound their
way through St James's Park to Buckingham Palace. A huge chant
began. 'We want the King' over and over until at last, the balcony
doors opened and out came the Royal family. Another great roar of
singing and laughing. By this time it was 6 pm and the doors opened
again, and the Royal family and Mr Churchill came out to cheers
and roars from the crowds. To this day I still do not know how he
could have got from Whitehall to the Palace, but there he was. It
was a blazing hot day. I cannot even remember eating or drinking

at all. Spent all evening around the Palace. Must have looked good from inside.

It gradually became twilight and the Palace was floodlit for the first time. The balcony doors opened again to the roars of the crowd. Who ever imagined going home? We lived thirty miles from London. Midnight and Big Ben chimed and the Royal family came out again for the last time.

After living in hope of another view, the crowd drifted off in to St James's and Green Park. It was a lovely warm night and we all lay out on the grass and slept. As soon as it was daylight (around 4 am) Leslie and myself and thousands more walked up the Mall as by this time everyone was ravenous. We walked back to Liverpool Street and found a café open around 7 am. We had tea and toast and realised how hungry we were.

Got back to Chelmsford around midday. A note from Leslie's department saying, 'where was you?' and please report as soon as possible. I went back to work the next day and were all informed that the war was not over in the Far East. It was hard to settle down to work with the beautiful summer days outside.

By this time Leslie asked me to marry him, against my dad's wishes. So one weekend at the end of July they were on holiday in Bournemouth, we packed our bags and moved up to London finding a flat in South West London. I also got a job in Fleet Street. I heard from my sister Rene, that there was a Court Summons to make me return to the factory. As she was the only one who knew my address, nothing was heard about it. The war in the Far East dragged on until August. I went out to buy a paper with screaming headlines 'Atom Bomb Dropped on Two Towns in Japan, with hundreds of thousands killed.' How we cheered, Japan surrendered, the date I cannot remember. More celebrations around the Palace, this time we had somewhere to walk back to. The days went into weeks and everything settled down.

My sister's boyfriend came back to England briefly and promised to send for her. By this time she had also left home staying with an Aunt in Southend. One cold windy night in March after clearing all the papers and dollars sent from John, we met at Euston for the night train to Glasgow and thence to Prestwick for a flight to the USA. This was March 1946 and I did not see her again until 1962. She wrote of the wonderful food and fruit stores and sent my dad food parcels.

Leslie and I bought a little house in South East London and were very happy. I sent my dad the address and he and my stepmother came up to see us one weekend.

I bought bits of second hand furniture as all new furniture was controlled by dockets and you could only qualify if you had children and were bombed out. We managed a bed, table, armchairs and brought them back in three journeys with a barrow. This seemed the end of my war. I married Leslie, had three girls, Vanessa, Juanita and Julia, and moved house around every three years.

We eventually moved back to Chelmsford and in 1961 I found work as an auxiliary nurse in the local hospital. Eventually did my training as a 'mature student' and am still working in 1995 as a trained nurse.

I am now 81 years of age and the grandmother of eight grandchildren. And so life goes on.

Olive's story is a truly remarkable account of her life and the part that she played in making history. Reading about her wartime work and her personal life, intertwined against the backdrop of the war as it painstakingly rumbled on, was a joy to read.

I have mentioned elsewhere in this book regarding people going about their everyday lives, whatever that might have involved, whilst dealing with the added dynamic of the war going on in the background; Olive's story was a good example of what this meant.

Olive's journey begins with her wanting to join the ATS and her father saying 'no'. However, he then allows her to go and work with him at Hoffmann's, which in some respects was an even more dangerous role. It looks at her personal life, the choice she makes between Dennis and Leslie, and the affect that has on her father and stepmother, or more a case of their reaction. How would 'becoming acquainted' with each other have been seen if this was the time of the First World War? The time she described in minute detail of going up to London to join in with the celebrations for the end of the war in Europe, was truly spellbinding. It is interesting that Olive's journey started and finished in Chelmsford. Her story began with her as a single girl aged 25, still doing what her father told her to, but in the space of five years she had blossomed in to a woman, ready and willing to make her own decisions, leaving home with Leslie because her father had refused his permission for them to marry.

An interesting footnote to Olive's story is that when she spoke of her sister Rene going off to start a new life in America, what she didn't say was that Rene was eight months pregnant at the time.

CHAPTER SIX

Famous Women from Chelmsford

Most towns in the United Kingdom boast individuals who from humble beginnings have gone on to achieve greatness, fame or even infamy. For some this might be in sport, while others excel at music, art, fashion, writing, the military, education, policing, nursing or politics. The list could almost be endless.

April Cantelo was born on 2 April 1928 in Purbrook, Hampshire. She spent her secondary education as a pupil at the Chelmsford High School for Girls, and left there determined to become an accomplished opera singer. She was a pupil at the school between 1939 and 1946, while two of the school's other notable pupils, Mary Humphrys and Margaret Anstee, were also there. After leaving school April studied in London under the likes of Czech conductor and composer Vilem Tausky, who was the musical director of the Carl Rosa Opera Company between 1945 and 1949, Joan Cross, who was a soprano who during the Second World War undertook the direction of the Sadler's Wells Theatre Company, and Imogen Holst, who was an English-born composer, arranger, conductor and teacher. She was also the only child of the internationally acclaimed composer, Gustav Holst. All three were established stars of many years standing.

April's journey as an opera singer saw her perform with the Glyndebourne Chorus, before making her solo debut in 1950 at Edinburgh, as Barbarina and Echo. During the early 1950s she sang at Covent Garden Opera House on numerous occasions, again singing Barbarina, and also Countess Ceprano and Poussette.

She went on to appear in many of the world's most acclaimed operatic pieces, including playing:

Manon Lescaut in *Boulevard Solitude*
Jenny in *Rise and Fall of the City of Mahogany*
Lady in *The Grace of Todd*
Susan in *Dinner Engagement*
Orpha in *Ruth*
Helena in *A Midsummer Night's Dream*
Bertha in *The Violins of Saint-Jaques*
Beatrice Weston in *Our Man in Havana*
Swallow in *The Happy Prince*
Ann in *Julius Caesar Jones*
Semele in *Semele*

April continued to appear on stage throughout her career, performing with numerous different choirs and orchestras, including the choir of King's College, Cambridge and the Royal Philharmonic Orchestra. She married the distinguished conductor, Colin Davis, in 1949. They had two children, Christopher and Suzanne, but divorced in 1964. Davis was appointed a CBE in 1965 and was knighted in 1980.

When Mary Kenyon was a pupil at Chelmsford High School for Girls she was Mary Humphrys, born in Ilkeston in Derbyshire, who grew up in Nottinghamshire, the daughter of Claude and Mary Humphrys. Her father Claude was a captain in the Royal Navy, but when he retired he bought a fruit farm in Essex, which resulted in Mary attending Chelmsford High School for Girls, her first day being in April 1934. During her time there she fully immersed herself in school life, becoming a prefect, house captain twice, school captain, sub-editor of the school's magazine, as well as treasurer of the school's social literary club.

Mary appears to have been a well-liked student who was well thought of by her teachers. Not only was she academically bright, she also had a pleasant demeanour as well as an engaging personality.

Her sister Patricia was also a pupil at the school, starting there on the same day.

During the Second World War, trenches had been dug in the grounds of the school where the girls would shelter in the event of a German air raid on the town. During such times the headmistress, Miss Geraldine Cadbury, was known to provide sweets for the children, joined on some occasions by Mary in her capacity as head girl.

Mary's time at Chelmsford High School for Girls came to an end in July 1941 when she completed her secondary education. All her hard work meant that she was accepted to study English at Somerville College, Oxford, becoming the first pupil from the school to attend Oxford. All previous University-bound girls from Chelmsford had gone to either Cambridge or London. She was tutored by John Ronald Reuel Tolkien, better known as J.R.R. Tolkien, the well-known author of *The Hobbit* and *The Lord of the Rings*. He was also a noted poet and philologist, who had served as a lieutenant with the Lancashire Fusiliers during the bloody fighting of the First World War, surviving the Battle of the Somme in 1916.

Somerville Hall was founded in 1879, and it didn't become Somerville College until 1894. It was named after the Scottish mathematician and scientist Mary Somerville, an intellectual in an age opposed to women pursuing academic careers.

Because of the war, Mary's course was reduced to two years by the government, but she still passed, receiving a BA in English. Besides having to contend with her studies she was also required by the University to undertake twelve hours of community work per week, in support of the war effort on the home front. Mary became an air-raid warden.

At the end of the course in 1943, Mary and her fellow students, who had acquired their degrees, were informed that they would be required to serve their country and help with the war effort. To this end a be-suited gentleman from the Foreign Office attended Somerville College and spoke to the young women, some of whom he was hoping to recruit. He spoke about them being needed 'for vital work of national importance, total secrecy'. Mary was one of those who was more than happy to take up the challenge, whatever it might be.

Mary soon found herself working at the British government's Code and Cypher School facility at Bletchley Park in Buckinghamshire, where she was one of those tasked with decoding the now famous Enigma transmissions in Hut 6, where Alan Turing, the person who actually cracked the Enigma code, also worked.

Enigma machines were what Germany and her allies used to send secret Morse-coded radio communications, which meant that being able to break the codes would provide Britain and her allies with vital information about what actions Germany was planning. Dwight D. Eisenhower, the Supreme Allied Commander, deemed the eventual cracking of the Enigma code as having been vital to the eventual Allied victory in the Second World War.

Mary worked at Bletchley Park from the summer of 1943 until the end of the war in Europe in May 1945. According to the Bletchley Park website, she was employed in the Registration Room, collecting, collating and organising signals. The staff at Bletchley Park worked hard. They worked a six-day week, which consisted of three different shifts: 1600 hours to midnight, midnight to 0800 hours, and 0800 hours to 1600 hours, with only a thirty-minute break per shift worked. The unsocial hours affected most, one way or another. The work was extremely repetitive, but required absolute focus and concentration, as missing a single piece of information could literally cost somebody their life. For many it was a case of work, eat and sleep: even on their day off, they were usually so tired that all they did was sleep. Staff had a total of four weeks' leave in a year, which could be taken in periods of a week at a time.

Mary's time at Bletchley Park came to a sudden and abrupt end. On 8 May 1945, VE Day, she was allowed time off from her duties to attend a friend's wedding. On her return she was refused entry, and that was the end of that particular chapter of Mary's life. Mary did not tell her family about her wartime exploits until the 1980s, by which time her father was dead. He would have certainly been proud of what his daughter had quietly achieved and the part she had played during the war.

Bletchley Park, which had numerous cover names during the war, including 'Station X', 'HMS Pembroke V' and 'BP', to name but a few, was actually owned by Admiral Sir Hugh Sinclair, head of the Secret Intelligence Service, or MI6 as it is known today. He had purchased the property in May 1938 for £6,000 of his own money, to be used by the Government Code and Cypher Schools and the Secret Intelligence Service in the event of war. Was that just a lucky guess on Sir Hugh's part, or a strong belief in what was to come?

After the war Mary returned to civvy street, with none of her family or friends having the slightest clue what she had been doing for the previous two years. She took up work with the publishing company Eyre & Spottiswoode, where she worked with the well-known novelist Graham Greene. The publisher still exists to this day. She met a writer and music critic by the name of Max Kenyon, whom she married in 1948, and they had three children, daughters Corinna and Susanna, and son Charles.

Mary kept her ties with the Chelmsford High School for Girls. One of her daughters, Susanna, was also a pupil at the school. In the 1970s Mary became the chairman of the school's Old Girls, and in 1982 she published a book entitled, *A History of Chelmsford County High School*.

Mary passed away in 2017 at the age of 94, having led a full and interesting life. An obituary appeared in *The Guardian* newspaper dated Sunday 12 February 2017, written by her son Charles.

Margaret Joan Anstee was born in Chelmsford, Essex on 25 June 1926 and in 1937, at the age of eleven, she became a pupil at Chelmsford High School for Girls, where she remained until 1944. Hers was a normal upbringing. Her mother looked after Margaret, her siblings and the family home, while her father who was a typesetter, worked for a local company. After leaving the school she continued her studies at Newnham College, which was part of Cambridge University, graduating from there in 1947 with first-class honours in French and Spanish. Even then it was not clear that she would go on to become one of Chelmsford High School for Girls' most renowned and notable students.

In 1948, just a year after finishing her studies at Cambridge University, she joined the Foreign Office, where she was appointed to the Latin American department, although she was quickly informed that a woman would not be sent to the region, in case they might succumb to a local man.

By 1951 she had moved on and was working for the head of the American Section, a man by the name of Donald Maclean. Does the name ring a bell? It should do, as he defected to the Soviet Union. Despite his defection, the sensitive nature of his work, and the fact that they had worked together, Margaret was never questioned about him.

In the early 1950s the Foreign Office had a policy that barred female employees from marrying. Those who chose to do so were forced to resign. Margaret fell foul of this policy and was forced to resign when she decided to marry a colleague in 1951. Her husband was posted to Singapore and the Philippines in 1952, and Margaret went with him, but sadly the marriage did not last. She would later famously say 'He took to Manila life like a duck to water, but unfortunately failed to stick to water.'

On her return to England in late 1952 she started working for the United Nations, and was even offered a job by the United Nations Technical Assistance Board, working in Mexico, but this appointment was vetoed by the 'head of mission' due to Margaret being a woman.

After becoming the United Nations' first female field officer, her work, which was mainly in poor developing countries throughout Africa and South America, took her to over 130 different countries, 15 of which she lived in. She was responsible for coordinating the United Nations humanitarian responses to disasters all over the world.

Margaret developed a particular attachment to Bolivia and its people after she became the deputy resident representative there in 1960, eventually building her own house on the shores of Lake Titicaca. General Pinochet's bloody takeover of the country in

1973 was something she found particularly distasteful, although, maybe fortunately for her, she was not in the country at the time he seized power.

She eventually became the first female Assistant Secretary General at the United Nations in 1974, under Kurt Waldheim, an appointment which made her the most senior female of that organisation.

As a person she was passionate and determined, a free spirit who spoke her mind, even if it was against the United Nations. In a male-dominated working environment her approach wasn't always appreciated, but that didn't hold her back, and in 1987 she was made the Director-General of what was known as the United Nations' third headquarters, in Vienna, whose main work consisted of a targeted approach against those individuals involved in drug trafficking. The Vienna office was also the Centre for Social Development and Humanitarian Affairs.

In 1993, which was her final year of working for the United Nations, she was also the Secretary-General's Special Representative to Angola, as well as the first woman to head a United Nations peace-keeping mission.

Her work for the United Nations saw her come into contact with some of the world's most noted and hard to reach politicians and leaders, in her attempts at making the world a better and safer place for everybody.

After working for the United Nations for forty-one years, Margaret didn't stop, she carried on in a similar vein, utilising the years of experience she had amassed working for the UN. In 1994 Margaret was made a Dame Commander of the Most Distinguished Order of St Michael and St George in the New Year Honours list. She was also honoured by the governments of Austria, Bolivia and Morocco.

She also found time to write five books:

1970 – *Gate of the Sun: A Prospect of Bolivia*
1996 – *Orphan of the Cold War: The inside story of the collapse of the Angolan Peace Process 1992–1993*

2003 – *Never Learn to Type: A Woman in the United Nations* (Her memoirs)
2009 – *The House on the Sacred Lake* (Her life in Bolivia)
2013 – *An Unlikely Spanish Don – The Life and Times of Professor John Brand Trend*

This is a potted history of Margaret's life and achievements. But it still provides a comprehensive picture of how an ordinary girl, from an ordinary family from Chelmsford, went on to achieve extraordinary things through hard work, a passion for what she did and sheer determination to finish what she had begun. Margaret was a trailblazer, who did not believe that the world of commerce and politics was a place where only men could succeed.

Even though nearly all of her working achievements occurred after 1950, her story, as far as Chelmsford is concerned, really began when she was an 11-year-old schoolgirl starting her secondary education at Chelmsford High School for Girls in 1937.

Dame Margaret Anstee died on 25 August 2016, at the age of ninety. In a message given by the then Secretary-General of the United Nations, Ban Ki-moon, before her funeral, he paid her the following compliment:

> Right up until the end of her life, Margaret Anstee called for greater international cooperation and collective action for peace, sustainable development and human rights.
>
> She was a true global citizen whose career is a powerful testament to the power of individuals to make a difference in the world.

A more genuine eulogy would be hard to find. An obituary appeared in the *Daily Telegraph* on 28 August 2016, recounting her life and achievements.

Rosemary Vercoe was born on 29 April 1917 at Ealing in London. She was the second of five children born to Doctor Richard Herbert Vercoe and his wife, Elizabeth Selina Vercoe.

Rosemary went on to become an actress and costume designer of some renown, eventually working with the likes of Jonathan

Miller, the famous English theatre and opera director and actor. He was also a doctor, TV presenter and appeared in *Beyond the Fringe* with Peter Cook and Dudley Moore.

Rosemary was educated at the Chelmsford High School for Girls, before moving on to the Chelsea School of Art, where one of her teachers was Henry Moore, who was perhaps best known for his abstract sculptures. The London District Theatre Unit was where she found her first job, working as both an actress and costume designer, before moving on to the Players' Theatre costume department during the Second World War, which had opened at 43 King Street, Covent Garden, London, on 18 October 1936. It was known for producing period-style musical comedies, and just over a year later it also introduced Victorian-style music hall productions. Some of the thespians who acted for the theatre included Hattie Jacques, Peter Ustinov and Clive Dunn.

After the end of the war Rosemary moved on to work for the Shakespeare Memorial Theatre in Stratford-upon- Avon, where she was the costume designer for their production of *The Taming of the Shrew*. She toured with the same company when they travelled to Australia in 1949–50, as an understudy actress and costume designer. She was meticulous in her attention to detail, and would rather find everyday clothes of the time she needed, rather than design and make a costume.

Rosemary married Patrick Robertson, a set designer with whom she had collaborated on numerous occasions. She died on 28 July 2013 at the Highgate Nursing Home in Islington, London.

CHAPTER SEVEN

Education

Education in schools as we know it today can be traced back to around 1837. Rural areas, which accounted for most of the country outside of the big towns and cities, provided schooling for the children of its working-class residents. Such schools were founded on the strength of charitable funding from what were known as 'societies'. These societies became eligible for Government funding, but not all society run schools jumped at the opportunity, because they felt that to do so would compromise their independence. From 1839, those schools who accepted the government's funding also had to let the schools be scrutinised by inspectors. If they weren't happy with the school's curriculum, then the funding was withdrawn. By the 1860s, the total annual amount that the government provided for education was £800,000.

The year 1844 saw the birth of what were called 'ragged schools'. These were charitable organisations who provided free education for destitute children in working-class districts up and down the country. Besides education, these schools also provided clothing, food, and lodging.

The teachers who worked in these schools were, in almost all cases, volunteers. The 'schools' were not purpose built, far from it, classrooms varied, but could be in such locations as a stable, a loft, or even a railway arch. It is believed the term 'ragged' came from the children who attended such schools being raggedly dressed, and most not even in possession of shoes.

The ragged schools had some prominent supporters, two in particular stood out. Anthony Ashley-Cooper, the 7th Earl of Shaftesbury, who was one of Britain's greatest social reformers, which included his interests in education. He went on to serve as the President of the London Ragged School Union for thirty-nine years, such was his commitment to the organisation.

Charles Dickens first became associated with ragged schools in 1843, when he visited the Field Lane Ragged School, which was situated in the notorious Saffron Hill slum near Farringdon, in central London. He was so appalled at what he saw during that visit that he was inspired to write *A Christmas Carol*. It is also claimed that the area of Field Lane was the setting for Fagin's den in *Oliver Twist*.

As an aside, but in keeping with Dickens' *Oliver Twist,* Chelmsford had a number of what were known as 'Industrial Schools', which were for the education and training of destitute boys, having been first established in 1872. The boys who attended these schools did so voluntarily, but they had to be unconvicted of having committed crime, although they could also be directed to attend these schools under the order of a magistrate. Part of the boys' time was then spent in school, whilst the rest of their time would be spent working, in such roles as gardening, housework, cobbler, or tailoring.

The locations of these schools in Chelmsford were the Essex Industrial School for Boys, Baddow Road and the Industrial School for Destitute Boys, Primrose Hill, which later became the Essex Industrial School & Home for Destitute Boys. Each of the schools catered for well over 100 boys.

What was noticeable by their absence, was a lack of any similar facilities for girls in Chelmsford, which goes a long way to emphasizing the attitude towards females in general.

Another of the supporters of the Ragged Schools, was Angela Burdett-Coutts, of the Coutts banking family. She was one of the wealthiest women of Victorian times, and gave large sums of money to the Ragged Schools Union.

The 1860s saw the birth and rise of what were known as parish schools, which were jointly funded with charitable donations and affordable subscriptions for parents to pay, which was usually a minimal amount and one that was affordable by most. There was a certain amount of resistance by some parents to their children having any form of education, especially girls, as they would rather have them out earning money for the family or looking after the home. In relation to girls, there was a belief that educating them was a complete and utter waste of time. After all why did they need to know how to read and write, or anything to do with history, art, science or Latin, when all they were going to be doing in life was looking after the home, cooking and cleaning, getting married and having children?

In parish schools the curriculum was largely religious based, and was usually delivered by the local curate of the parish church, and stuck to the fundamentals of reading, writing and arithmetic. Despite this push to education, it was more limited for girls than it was for boys, because when they grew up it was very rare for them to have careers, and those women who proved to be intellectually bright enough came up against ignorance, as most professions simply wouldn't allow women to join them. In 1868 the Taunton Royal Commission's report on secondary education highlighted the limitations of schooling for females. Oddly enough the one profession that they were allowed into was teaching, but it was perceived as a low-status occupation, that wasn't particularly well paid.

It could be suggested that the government was simply trying to ensure a standardisation in the education that was being provided to the nation's children. It could equally be argued that the reason for the government offering such funding in the first place was to ensure that the children's minds were not being indoctrinated with material of a subversive nature.

Education was obviously high on the government's agenda because between 1870 and 1880, there were three education Acts – The Education Act 1870, the Education Act 1876 and the Education Act 1880, the last of which was the real game changer, as it specifically made school attendance compulsory between the ages of 5 and 10, not necessarily because it wanted all children to have a proper education, but rather to stop children being used by unscrupulous employers who were happy to pay for their child labour. Making education compulsory had actually evolved as a result of recommendations put forward as a result of the Royal Commission on the Factories Act 1876.

By 1899 the upper age limit for compulsory education had risen to 12.

Compulsory education included children who were blind and deaf as per legislation brought in under the Elementary Education (Blind and deaf Children) Act 1893, and six years later this was added to for children who were physically impaired, under the Elementary Education (Defective and Epileptic Children) Act 1899.

Despite the commencement of these Acts, attendance, although high, was not as might be assumed, running at 100 per cent. For parents it was a case of simple mathematics. They could either have their children out working and bringing much-needed money in to the family home, or let them attend school, and not only then miss out on the monies that their children could be earning, but have to pay for them to get an education. For most, it was a simple choice.

The requirement for parents to contribute towards their child's education was stopped in 1891, when a change in the law made all education free. Because parents were still reliant on their children bringing money into the home, many children continued to work outside of their school hours, this included before and after they had attended school for the day, and by the beginning of the twentieth century, truancy had become a major problem.

In the late 1830s, early 1840s, the Parish Workhouse in East Hanningfield ceased to be, and moved to new premises in Chelmsford town centre. However, the old building didn't go to waste, it became what was known as a Dame School, the person in charge of the new school being a headmistress by the name of

Bathsheba Cheek. The building remained in place until 1865 when it was demolished. The building which replaced it was also used for educational purposes, and was one of a number of new National Schools.

In essence a Dame School was a form of private elementary school, a school where children experienced their first school years and received their primary education.

Dame Schools weren't unique to England, they could be found in most English speaking countries at the time. The teachers were usually women and a lot of the schools were in fact their homes. But as the one at East Hanningfield, Chelmsford, shows, that was not always the case. They were not an invention of the nineteenth century, as references to them have been found in different texts going back to the sixteenth century.

They didn't necessarily have a good reputation, with little or no restriction placed upon those who decided to open such schools, but for the poorest of society, they served a purpose.

Chelmsford High School for Girls is a prestigious grammar school that is over 100 years old. During the period 1850–1950 girls who received a good education were much more likely to be from affluent families. A woman from a well-to-do family was expected to have a certain level of education, as this reflected well on her family and made it easier to marry her off. Wealthier families did not need their children to go out to work to bring in money either, and could afford shoes, clothes and books to support their children's education. After the First World War women's aspirations for their own lives were changed, partly in response to the war itself – for many, marriage was no longer an option as so many young men had been killed in the war – and partly because war work on the home front had given them an opportunity to participate in the workforce in a new way. Thus some women now wanted a career, and for this they would need a good education.

The official opening of the County High School for Girls, Chelmsford, took place on Wednesday 1 May 1907 at 3.30pm, and was conducted by Sir William Anson, the Liberalist Unionist MP for Oxford University, although the first pupils were not admitted until the following Monday, 6 May 1907. Between 1850 and 1950 the school had three headmistresses.

Miss Mabel F. Vernon Harcourt was the first headmistress and was present when the school was officially opened on 1 May 1907. At the time there were just seventy-six pupils enrolled at the school, which catered for children between the ages of 9 and 18.

During her tenure, the school magazine first appeared. She resigned her position as headmistress in December 1910, shortly before her marriage to Mr William Arthur Price. It was common for women to give up their jobs when they married. Society expected that they would have children and look after the family home. There was a stark choice for women between having a career and marrying and having a family life; living with a partner, or continuing to work after marriage, was frowned upon.

At the time of her marriage, Mabel, who was 36 years of age, was living at 16 Maltese Road, Chelmsford, and was a spinster. Her husband, William Arthur Price, a widower, was 50 years of age, a consultant mechanical engineer and living in Oxford, which was where Mabel was born. William's first wife, Edith Octavia Price, died in 1907 when she was 42 years of age.

The couple were married at St Giles parish church, Oxford, on 28 December 1910. The 1911 census, which was taken on Sunday, 2 April 1911, showed that the marital home was at 135 Sandyford Road, Newcastle-upon-Tyne. William brought with him to the marriage three children, Penelope, who was 15 years of age, Edith who was 13, and a son John, who was 5. There were also four servants, including a cook, housemaid, parlour maid and a nurse.

Mabel died aged 91, on 11 October 1965 at Brookfurlong Farm, Islip, Oxfordshire. William had passed away on 13 May 1954, aged 94, at the Oketon Nursing Home, Teddington, London. He left £10,460 15s 5d, not to his wife Mabel, but to Owen Price, a lieutenant colonel in the British army, and Francis Vernon Price, a university lecturer. I assume that these were his sons, possibly from his marriage to Mabel.

Miss Edith Maud Bancroft was born on 4 July 1870, in Kingswood near Bristol. She was the youngest of four children, three of whom were Sarah Elizabeth Hessel's from her marriage to William Hessel. Edith was the only child of Sarah's marriage to Reuben Bancroft. Edith's eldest half-brother, Robert, was already 15 years of age when she was born.

It appears that Edith's parents married in July 1869, a year before Edith was born. Sarah and her first husband, William had lived in Australia for a time, as their second son, William, was born in Sydney in 1860, ten years before Edith was born.

Edith became the school's second headmistress when she took over from Mabel Harcourt. She was 31 years of age when she began her tenure in January 1911, one would imagine immediately on the return of the school's pupils after the Christmas holiday.

The 1911 census shows Edith living at 16 Maltese Road, Chelmsford. The property had previously been occupied by Mabel Frances Vernon, during her time as the school's headmistress.

Such was Edith's position as headmistress that she had two servants. Ellen Wild was her housekeeper, while Gwendoline Emily, who was only 15 years of age, was her domestic housemaid.

Edith had the unenviable task of leading the school through the difficult years of the First World War. The constant worry about what would happen if a wayward German bomb should fall on the school must have given Edith sleepless nights throughout the war.

Miss Geraldine Cadbury became the school's third headmistress on the retirement of Miss Edith Bancroft in 1935. She remained in post until 1961. Like her predecessor, she had been in charge of the school during a time of war. There had been massive advances in technology since the First World War, especially in relation to weaponry, equipment and aircraft. The open-topped biplanes and Zeppelins had been replaced by Messerschmidts and Stukas.

Below is a copy of a letter that Miss Cadbury sent out to parents regarding air raids.

County High School
Chelmsford
22 October 1940

Arrangements for Air Raids continuing after
School Hours

I shall be glad if you will let me know in writing which of the three alternatives below you wish your daughter to follow if an air raid goes on after the normal time for closing school.

1. If you are prepared to leave it to my discretion to release your daughter when it appears to be safe to do so in order that she can go home.
2. If you wish to send or call for your daughter. If so, please let me know who you are authorising to fetch her.
3. If you wish her to remain in the school trench until the all clear signal is given.

You will realize that neither the Education Committee nor the Headmistress, nor the staff can accept responsibility for any accident that may occur as a result of raids either in the school or on the journey home, and I shall be glad if you will state in writing that you clearly understand this point; and that you will take responsibility for your daughter leaving school either alone or with an authorised person, in the case of alternatives 1 or 2.

Yours sincerely
G.M. Cadbury
Headmistress

Although the school was not directly targeted, as it was of no military value, and served no military purpose, it did suffer during the war when German bombers missed their targets or jettisoned bombs they no longer needed. There was such an incident in December 1944, and although nobody was hurt or killed, many of the school's windows were cracked or smashed. Doors were blown open and areas of the roof and brickwork were damaged.

Throughout all of this upheaval and disruption, the girls dealt with the situation admirably. There were numerous occasions when pupils and staff had to take refuge in the school shelters or trenches. Despite the disruption this caused to lessons and exams, school life carried on as best it could in the circumstances.

Miss Edith Maud Bancroft wrote the following in the school's autumn term report in 1919. It is dated 27 September 1919, nearly a year after the end of the First World War.

> My experience with the majority of parents during the last year has made me realise that the quickened public interest in education and faith in its efficiency, are now affording us as educationalists, great opportunities which we must not fail to use. On the other hand, in some cases there is a greater laxity of home discipline which makes that of the school still more indispensable. This shows itself in many ways, in making requests to the school for frequent casual absences for pleasure, in allowing the children to attend late parties, and frequent cinemas in the midst of term, and the freedom too unrestricted out of doors. Against these, especially the first, the school is bound in the interests of the children, to raise its protest. In the great majority of cases I receive the loyal and warm cooperation of the parents, in many others my protest, once made is heeded, but the consensus of opinion and strong support on the part of all those in educational authority is necessary to save the children from these hindrances to proper work and to fit training of character.

This is a good example of a head teacher genuinely caring about her pupils' well being and wanting the best possible education for the girls under her direction.

Reports of speech day at the school in 1940 make for interesting reading, because they contain so much information about the school in wartime. Usually the headteacher would address such matters as pupil numbers, the school's academic and sporting achievements, building work or staff changes. But these were not normal times. Thus topics included the blacking out of the school's windows, the need for trenches to be dug in the school grounds, underground bunkers and gas masks.

The aim of the headmistress and her staff was to make everyday life as normal as possible for the pupils. Although the Second World War was just twenty years after the end of the First World War, talking about and having to consider such issues was not part of the normal brief of a headteacher.

The school had not been able to reopen for the beginning of the school year in September 1939 until the headmistress had arranged for the digging of trenches in the school grounds. In fact, the school did not finish the first of the required trenches until 8 November 1939, which prevented the school from fully reopening until the end of that month. The issue of not being able to sufficiently black out all of the school's windows meant the need to cut out evening parties, plays and concerts.

Many of the girls who left Chelmsford High School for Girls for the last time in June 1940 went on to have enjoyable careers. Four went to university. This required not only academic ability, but also financial support from willing parents who understood the importance of educating their daughters to achieve their potential. Several of the year group had decided on a career in education and left the school to attend teacher training colleges. One student went to train in horticulture, while another studied to become a pharmacist. Several students went to work in the laboratories connected to local hospitals. A number of girls went into nursing, both in a civilian capacity and with the armed forces, while others took up different kinds of war-related work. One young lady, Margaret Marriage, went to work in London as a police officer, which was a new career open to women.

In 1942 the school's speech day successes were described in two ways. Firstly, the chosen careers of pupils who had left the school in May 1942 were listed, along with some of the achievements of girls who had left the school in previous years. Several girls left to join the armed services, with a number taking up nursing. Others had opted to do work for the Women's Volunteer Service. One particular ex-pupil, Fay Neely, joined the Women's Royal Naval Service, but only after she had initially obtained a position as assistant housekeeper at Sherborne School in Dorset. Other members of staff left for numerous different reasons connected to the war, and very quickly Fay found herself with a greatly depleted staff, which meant her having to cook for 120 people, three times a day. She then left to do her bit for the war effort.

Margaret Lanning, who had worked at the War Office since 1940, passed the Civil Service Intermediate Diploma in French and then went on to take a course to become a laboratory assistant in the Ministry of Supply Research Laboratories. She hoped to progress even further.

Several old girls had continued with their studies and gone on to further education, achieving a series of passes in different fields, including the pharmaceuticals industry and the Society of Radiographers.

Between 1943 and 1946, the school's May speech day was littered with similar anecdotes about academic and work-based achievements by ex-pupils, which proved to be an extremely impressive list for both the school and the individuals concerned.

Chelmsford is also the home to the New Hall School, whose motto today is, *'The Best Start in Life.'* It is one of the oldest Catholic schools in the United Kingdom, having been on its current site in Chelmsford since 1799, and was founded by the Canonesses of the Holy Sepulchre, a religious community founded by Susan Hawley in 1642. The school provided girls with a Catholic education, which in a predominantly Protestant country of the day, was one that was hard to find. Not surprisingly its teachings were of a religious nature, and focused on prayer, life in the community, being of service to others and hospitality.

The school's buildings have their own unique history, and at different times the Tudor Palace of Beaulieu has been owned by King Henry Vlll, Mary Tudor, Elizabeth l, Earl of Sussex, and Oliver Cromwell.

All in all, the examples set out in the above paragraphs show what young women could achieve in life, having started out with a good education and then acquired high level and well-paid careers and professions. Coming from affluent backgrounds obviously bestowed a certain privilege on these girls in comparison to other girls of the time, who would have experienced pressure to marry and have children, or to take lower-paid work in order to contribute to the family finances. There is no suggestion that children from working-class families did not have a good or positive work ethic. They simply could not earn enough money to break free of the social class they had been born into. Would young women from Chelmsford's less wealthy families have been able to succeed academically and create better lives for themselves if they had been able to have a better education? The answer is almost certainly yes.

While researching schools I looked at the number of girls shown as being in education in the Chelmsford area in the national censuses from 1851 to 1911. In the search engine I used the words, 'scholar', 'school', 'student' and 'pupil', to ensure that I had captured every possible Chelmsford female student.

In 1851, according to the census of England, there were fifteen girls from the Chelmsford area who were officially recorded as being in full-time education, at a school in Osborn Terrace, New London Road, Chelmsford: the headmistress was Sarah Ann Matson. As a comparison, there were only ten boys who were shown as being in education at the same time. The girls were: Cordelia Stiealfield, Emily Dettman, Olwea Spurgin, Rose Spurgin, Agatha Berebrow, Joanna Bostock, Rellina Salmon, Mary Goodrich Boys, Virginia Boys, Margaret Philbrick, Mary Heywood, Matilda Salt, Mary Salt, Henrietta Carwardine and Mary Cawardine.

The 1861 census records no girls being in education, showing that it wasn't high on the agenda of most families, especially working-class families. Most needed to have their children in work, earning money for the family, as soon as they possibly could.

In 1871 the census shows that there were twenty-seven girls in education in Chelmsford, specifically at Sutherland Lodge, in Baddow Road, Chelmsford. The headmistress was Miss Ellen Fitch. The girls were: Sally Bingess, Celia E. Burson, Katherine Dodd, Kate Allen, Amy E. Betcher, Frances M. Barwell, Frances L. Bewors, Emma B. Redmond, Catherine A. Harvey, Alice M. Caton, Annie Allen, Harriet A. Malo, Louisa E.M. Clarks, Emma L. Newman, Mary Richmond, Emily J. King, Rosa J. Barwell, Anna M. Taylor,

Margaret Harvey, Elizabeth R. Noyelk, Ada Fairhead, Mary E. Hawes, Ada S. Clarks, Charlotte L. Harvey, Gertrude M. King, Alice Quiller and Mary J. Hale. During the same period of time there were only five boys who were officially receiving an education at a school.

The 1881 census records that the following girls were pupils at a school in Tavistock House, New London Road, Chelmsford: Marion Adams, Mary Ann Arnold, C.H.J. Beader, Elizabeth Gertrude Beader, Jessie Grace Beader, Maria H. Cartley, Alice M. Dowsett, Ann L. Dowsett, Mary A. Dowsett, Mary Ann Hawkins, Martha Kidd, Edith Ruffle, Lillie Staples, Kate Hudson, Kate Staples, Kezia Orbell, Emily Orbell and Ilsa Von Mollier.

Surprisingly, the 1891 census held no records of girls in Chelmsford attending any educational establishments, and nor did the 1901 census. Perhaps the results were entered differently in those years and weren't found by my keyword searches.

The 1911 census records only nine girls who were born and lived in Chelmsford, aged between seven and fourteen years, as being in education. They were:

Rose Elizabeth Brazier, 7 Victoria Square, Victoria Road, Chelmsford.

Winifred Amy Brazier, 7 Victoria Square, Victoria Road, Chelmsford.

Gertrude Burton, 5 School View, Rainsford Road, Chelmsford.

Christie Curtis, 3 Victoria Road, Chelmsford.

Florence Curtis, 3 Victoria Road, Chelmsford.

Daisy Alice Hales, 45 Mildmay Road, Chelmsford.

Florence May Hawkes, 41 New Street, Chelmsford.

Violet Newman, 53 Victoria Road, New Street, Chelmsford.

Dorothy Louie Pedley, 4 London Road, Chelmsford.

As a direct comparison, only fourteen boys from Chelmsford were in the same age range, over the same period of time, and recorded as being in education.

Thinking these numbers seemed very low, I revisited the 1911 census, varying the search slightly, and came up with 873 girls' names who were showing as having been students in Chelmsford, so by 1911 many more girls were in school. Maybe this had something to do with the Old Age Pension Act 1908, which was enacted in January 1909 and gave people over the age of 70 a non-contributory old age pension of 5s a week, or 7s 6d for married couples. This directly affected more than half a million people. The pension ensured, overnight, that elderly people were no longer entirely dependent on their children in their twilight years. This was a burden which more often that not fell on the shoulders of daughters, especially those who had never married and remained living at home with their parents. Most of those who ended up being in receipt of these new government pensions, were women, rather than men. No longer having to provide for elderly dependants may have released family funds to pay for children's education.

Conclusion

How did life change for the women of Chelmsford between 1850 and 1950? And were all those changes for the better?

In the 1850s when a woman married she had almost no rights at all. If at the time of her marriage she owned property, all of it automatically became her husband's. If she owned land that rent was due on, those monies also became her husband's. A husband had the right to lock up his wife if she didn't do what he wanted. If he chose to beat her, she had no redress through the courts, all of which is absolutely staggering by today's standards. A woman's children were not even hers by law.

The right to a divorce in 1850 was controlled by the Church of England, the leaders of which looked upon divorce as a crime against God, which also meant that there was a massive social stigma attached to it. There were only three ways to officially separate. The first involved having the marriage annulled due to impotence, insanity or the possibility of incest. If the parties remarried and had children, the Church considered those offspring illegitimate.

A second way of obtaining a divorce was only available in cases of adultery, sodomy or physical violence, and although the couple could separate, they could not remarry. The third and final way was to obtain a separation and then sue the spouse through the courts. When and if a divorce was eventually granted, it did not make the couple's children illegitimate, but it was a long and expensive process, which was well out of reach for most people, as it was intended to be.

The Marriage & Divorce Act 1858 made matters slightly fairer for women, by allowing women who had not been divorced due to them having committed adultery, the right to custody of their children. The other extremely helpful aspect of the new Act was that such matters were taken away from the Church and placed with the civil courts, which helped take away some of the stigma which had previously been attached to the process.

More Acts of Parliament followed which helped address the imbalance between men and women, including the Married Women's Property Act of 1882.

Until the outbreak of the First World War, everyday life in England was class-based. Everyone knew their place in society and what was expected of them. Religion played a big part in people's lives, and marriage was between a man and a woman, with an expectation that children would be the outcome. It was the husband's role to go out to work and earn money to provide a roof over their heads, to put clothes on their backs and food on the table. It was the wife's job to stay at home, give birth to children and look after them, her husband and the home. The First World War changed everything as far as the social progression of women was concerned. All of a sudden they were needed to undertake jobs and work which had previously been the sole domain of men. During the bleak years between 1914 and 1919 they worked as bus drivers, taxi drivers and mechanics. They worked in munitions factories, they delivered the post, and many became nurses, while thousands of others undertook unpaid, but much needed, voluntary work. The majority of the members of the National Union of Women's Suffrage Societies supported the war and went as far as to keep an employment register so that the jobs of those who were serving in the armed forces could be filled by women. For the first time ever, women had a freedom that they had never known. They had their own money, their own friends, and they were not prepared to give it up. The money they were paid was more than they could have ever imagined, but it was a lot less than a man would have been paid to do the same job.

This understandably caused a problem, because men returning from fighting in the war were expecting their old jobs back, and their wives to return to what they had been before the war, but women had grown accustomed to their new-found independence. In 1918 more divorces were granted than ever before, and in 1919 there were even more. Numbers continued to increase before peaking in 1928.

The Representation of the People Act 1918 was passed into law to reform the electoral system throughout Great Britain and Ireland, which was a big plus for women. The Matrimonial Causes Act 1923 provided equality in divorce cases for men and women.

By the time of the Second World War life for women had changed drastically. In the twenty years since the end of the First World War, divorce had become more common. By 1945 divorces were five times higher in number than they had been in 1939. In 1946 the number had risen to 38,000, and by the end of 1947 that figure had increased drastically to 60,000. These are simply enormous increases which reflect the change, freedom and expectations of the time.

During the course of the Second World War, and specifically between 1942 and 1944, more than a million and a half American soldiers arrived in Great Britain, and by the time they left, they took with them some 60,000 British women who had become their wives. Times had certainly changed.

About the Author

Stephen is a happily retired police officer having served with Essex Police as a constable for thirty years between 1983 and 2013. He is married to Tanya who is also his best friend.

Both his sons, Luke and Ross, were members of the armed forces, collectively serving five tours of Afghanistan between 2008 and 2013. Both were injured on their first tour. This led to his first book; *'Two Sons in a Warzone – Afghanistan: The True Story of a Father's Conflict'*, which was published in October 2010.

His teenage daughter, Aimee, currently attends one of the District's secondary schools. Both of his grandfathers served in and survived the First World War, one with the Royal Irish Rifles, the other in the Mercantile Navy, whilst his father was a member of the Royal Army Ordnance Corps during the Second World War.

Stephen corroborated with one of his writing partners, Ken Porter on a previous book published in August 2012, *'German POW Camp 266 – Langdon Hills.'* It spent six weeks as the number one best-selling book in Waterstones, Basildon between March and April 2013. They have also collaborated on four books in the 'Towns & Cities in the Great War' series by Pen and Sword. Stephen has also written other titles for the same series of books.

Stephen co-wrote three crime thrillers which were published between 2010 and 2012, and centre around a fictional detective named Terry Danvers.

When he is not writing, Tanya and he enjoy the simplicity of walking their four German Shepherd dogs early each morning when most sensible people are still fast asleep in their beds.

Sources

www.thesuffragettes.org
www.spartacus-educational.com
www.britishnewspaperarchive.co.uk
www.essexregiment.co.uk
www.cwgc.co.uk
Wikipedia
www.redcross.org.uk
www.theguardian.com
www.cchs.co.uk
www.ww2history.com
www.openairclassroom.org.uk
www.missing-ancestors.com
www.encyclopedia.1914-1918-online.net
www.mylearning.org

Index

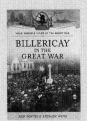

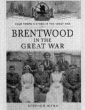
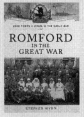
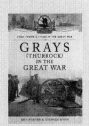

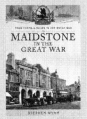

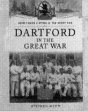

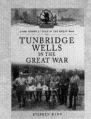

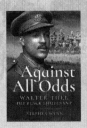